The Tapestry of Being

The Tapestry of Being

Talks on Practical Mysticism

Krishna Gauci

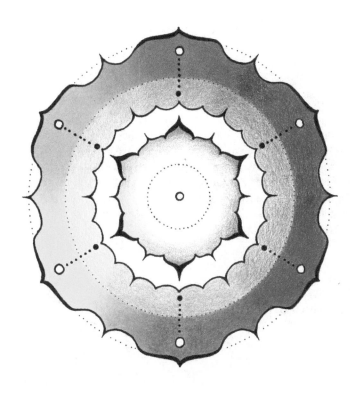

Tapestry of Being Press

Tapestry of Being Press
8621 SW 57th Avenue
Portland, OR 97219

Tapestryofbeing.org

Table of Contents

For the Master behind every Master

Preface:
The Nature of This Book

What you will be reading has been adapted from live teaching conversations and talks, and it still reflects the more informal style of its origin. You may find me repeating specific concepts and phrases. When I teach in person, this repetition is entirely intentional because I see that when we hear the same thing many times in different contexts, we retain it and understand it in new ways. I hope you will find that it serves the same purpose here.

Here are three ways you might approach what you read:

1. As a way to hold mutually contradictory spiritual teachings of the world in a universal context so that you can see them as part of a larger whole without having to change the teachings themselves.

2. As a manual of exercises, techniques, and practices that will give you a taste of different perspectives that can help you to develop in a variety of ways, no matter what picture of the universe you currently hold or who you now take yourself to be. You might like to have someone read them to you the first time you do each one. When you understand the Mandala orientation, you may see your own ways of using exercises from different sources to enrich your experience in the various nodes.

3. For those who may be looking for a non-sectarian
    template that you can use on your own or with oth-
    ers, this is an inclusive non-dual vision of reality that
    shows you ways to contact your internal guidance and
    develop uniquely in six essential dimensions. When I
    speak of the Tapestry of Being in this book, I refer to
    its teachings as an orientation, its Mandala as a tool,
    and its subject as your own life.

These teachings convey a way of relating to the mystery of
existence that is broad-minded, paradoxical, and intensely individual. There is a way in which we can allow perspectives to
have us and, in letting them enter us, they become something
unique to ourselves.

Acknowledgments

I want to thank Steve Beckett for recognizing the value that these teachings offer and his continuous support in helping me reach out to make them known. Through his prompting, I began presenting them more systematically, teaching courses and giving talks focused on the Mandala.

Both Steve and Anna Bruno continued to prod and encourage me to organize transcriptions of some of those talks into what has become this book. Steve continued to see this project through to its completion, and beyond.

I want to thank Margit Bantowsky for illustrating the Mandala. Beth Jenckes assisted with the initial draft, helping to organize the lectures into a logical sequence. Ellen Holmes contributed countless hours of editing work on the manuscript for which I'm very grateful. Michael Sanborn has also generously and patiently spent many hours doing the typesetting and covers, and his unwearied friendly professionalism has been invaluable.

And of course, my beloved wife Vivian Coles has been encouraging me throughout this process.

Finally, I want to thank those students who made it clear to me what a difference these teachings have made in their lives.

Introduction

An Orientation in Subjectivity

Today there are an endless variety of teachings, techniques, and practices promising spiritual awakening to help us live happier, more fulfilled lives. While this is great, it can also be confusing. On what basis do we know how to choose what serves us? Without a unifying center, how does it all hang together? We want to walk our own path, but we also want to make sure we are going somewhere worthwhile.

Our awakening is just the start of a road that no one before us has traveled. We do not need another program, but instead, an orientation in subjectivity. What does this mean?

In my case, after years of working with groups of people describing their own spiritual lives unfolding, a picture came into focus. There's a full spectrum of living that is potentially available to us, and perhaps this vision may give those who read this book a sense of what is possible to grow into, even among those who have already significantly awakened.

I began to understand this perspective intuitively long before I had words for it. The language about it emerged over time. I still feel that I have not found the perfect expression of it, but enough to begin to convey its essence.

The Tapestry orientation is the way that I came to relate to traditional spiritual understandings in a postmodern world. The foundation of this orientation developed from trying to make sense of my own direct experience and the experience of those I worked with without falling into a new dogmatism.

A Singular Vision with Depth Has Two Distinct Eyes

From my perspective, there are two intersecting experienced realities. They are two fundamental perspectives, or stances, or orientations to life, and they are both important in different ways.

I consider the subjective stance toward the Mystery of life to be the way of spirituality, while I consider the objective stance toward the Mystery of life to be the way of science.

This is not another form of reductionism or of what I would describe as "the fallacy of 50%." By that I mean it's not that reality is 50% subjective and 50% objective. Rather, it is that there are two distinct ways of seeing, and both of them are internally consistent. You can explain all subjective experience from an objective stance and proceed to describe 100% of reality from that perspective. Alternatively, you can explain all objective experience from a subjective stance and proceed to describe 100% of reality from that perspective. Each perspective sees what it sees—they are not the same—yet together they form the total experience of a single human being.

I think having two eyes is helpful for living a full life. I also think it's important to let them remain as two eyes and not try to make them somehow become one big eye. They are not one eye, and yet vision has a depth in the unforced and natural integration of the points of views of both eyes together.

From the objective perspective, I was born into a particular time and place. How do I know this? Because other people saw me, objectively, coming into the world, the doctors in the hospital and my mother told me this, and I accept it as objective truth. From this perspective, the world objectively existed before I arrived. That said, my actual direct subjective experience is that I was never born. I certainly don't remember being born. What I remember is the world slowly coming online one experiential piece at a time. There were sensations, colors, and sounds, and then from a rather timeless place there evolved a sense of myself as a center of attention in some particular place and time. At some point, my mother was looking in my direction and speaking to me. At another point, I was interacting with her.

From the subjective perspective I was a space of awareness and a time and place were found manifesting in my midst. Although being able to take the objective stance is a requirement for adulthood, I also have a direct experience of life that is subjective. In this very moment, everything is happening from the position of my own experience.

The phrase "subjective reality" has a pejorative connotation that I find makes us prejudiced about the level of respect it deserves. People hear the word "subjective" as if it means "inaccurate" (or at least "not trustable"). Whereas, people hear the word "objective" as if it automatically means "accurate and trustworthy."

Many of the advances in the world have been gleaned through being scientifically objective and provable objectively, but there's a whole other realm of experience that is the stuff of subjectivity such as art, love, and even meaning itself.

When I go to a doctor, I want someone who is objectively accurate in their assessment of me as a body, using what they see in front of them. But when I come home to my partner, I want to experience her in my subjectivity, and I want her to see me as a subject, too. I want heart-to-heart empathy.

The Tapestry of Being is a way of adapting to the mystery

called life, from the Radically Subjective perspective. In other words, it's from the ultimate first-person perspective. I will go into more detail on this in Chapter 2, but what I mean by this is different from, and yet related to, the usual notion of subjectivity. It is going deeper—to the heart of our existence, to what is prior to or beyond the ego/personality—and living life from that basis. Those who do this are not necessarily egoless, but they do know the Ground of their Being beyond the ego as their most profound, bedrock essential nature.

Not an Objective Cosmology

In this book, I will describe Unconditioned Awareness as being prior to, or "before," matter. On hearing me say this, someone once replied, "Well, we don't know what came first. We'd have to use a time machine to go before the Big Bang; we'd have to go there to see if Consciousness was there first." They misunderstood what I was saying.

I am not speaking in this book about any objective notions of the origins of the universe. Instead, I'm pointing to how, in immediate experience, there's a formless Awareness that is at the center or heart of our being, in every moment, even now. Arising within that formless Awareness is the feeling sensation of "I-am-ness" or "presence" that is the base of the experience of personal existence. So, this description is not about going back in time and seeing if there's a God at the beginning.

From an objective perspective, I am agnostic regarding whether there's a first Consciousness at the beginning of time. Quite honestly, I haven't seen any reason to believe it's necessary. Objectively speaking, from what I can see, there doesn't seem to be any proof of it. Evolution is a process of matter and energy, and—according to mainstream 21st century science—consciousness is merely epiphenomenal, something that is an activity of the material nervous system, the brain, electricity and internally integrated information networks. But for me, the jury's out on all of this. I'm also aware that there are researchers on the edges of neuroscience and maybe even quantum theory who may have more to say about "the hard problem" of the nature of consciousness. While I look at all their findings with great interest, I know that they, as scientists, are speaking from an objective perspective even if they conclude that everything is Consciousness. Whatever doubt or certainty they may have about their research is based upon looking at things objectively, from the second or third person perspective: the "exterior" or "outside" of experience.

In many mystic traditions, Consciousness is primary and matter proceeds as an emanation, unfolding or unpacking of the potential that's in Consciousness. They are not speaking from an objective perspective, but rather from direct, immediate, subjective experience and insight. The mystics speak from a meditational and visionary perspective, from going within, where they directly experience in themselves the origins of their nature.

These are two very different modes of research, and they are both important. The mystic traditions are not about reality from the objective perspective. My own experience of Divinity is that of The Ultimate Subjectivity, the great I AM, the Context of all experience.

I do not approach the claims of past spiritual traditions as if they were describing reality from the objective perspective. They were speaking from a time when objective science was not sufficiently developed to have what we now would consider accurate, objective explanations for reality. That is not to assume that scientific explanations today are perfect either, but we can move forward honoring the difference. Often traditional descriptions of the external universe were simply wrong. Sometimes, a respected spiritual person's internal or visionary experience could mistakenly be taken to be an objective truth. This is a confusion of perspectives.

In some cases, even ancient people realized this difference and did not consider explanations about objective reality from spiritual sources as always being literally true. There is a large corpus of traditional writings from around the world that understand religious stories or scriptures as being symbolic parables that describe internal subjective experiences.

The Tapestry of Being is a practical approach to teachings on the subjective dimension from different sources, times and cultures, and a way to make use of them now. It is about trusting that the vast subjective inheritance of humanity is worth exploring and using, even for those of us who are not allied with a single religious tradition. A large part of why I began teaching the Tapestry is that I found that people using non-dual spiritual teachings were often using many different processes without having a perspective that held those things together in a way that made sense in their totality.

I found that many of those people, like me, did not always want to have to choose just one particular worldview. Instead, they wanted to relate to life as it revealed itself to them, and yet to honor those who came before us and to receive what they have to offer.

So, the Tapestry is one larger context in which to find your way; it is a template, or a way of approaching things, rather than a map to follow.

How It Began for Me

When I was quite young, I experienced something that I could not share with anyone else. The experience repeated itself, and each time I did not speak of it to anyone.

I would be listening to another child describing something, telling me about their favorite toy or a game or some event; and as they were speaking, their words no longer had any meaning, and I became entranced. I became unable to follow their words. I'd found myself in a very, very, peaceful state, calm and filled with wellbeing.

As I slipped into this state, there was a relaxed listening, a delight in the sound of their voice, and then no recognition of the meaning of what they were saying. The room became filled with and transformed in, white light. The people and objects became covered in the shine of the light, and then everything was outshone and dissolved in its brilliance.

At this point there was a kind of gap, there was something that I can't speak about because I, as the speaker, wasn't there, but there was somehow a knowing of the "Nothingness."

There was no thinker. There was nothing I can describe except to say that there was only a total absence. I wasn't aware of it while it was happening. Just before it, I was conscious of the light. I was mindful of everything dissolving, but then there was no awareness of anything at all.

On coming out of this state, I did not return to the natural world. Instead, I found myself in a vast expansive cloud of conscious feeling, a realm of profound harmony. I was aware of being a part of an immeasurable unified field of energies. Although I experienced nothing but an ocean of bliss, I somehow knew that everyone and everything—every single person, every single thing—was that endless realm of expansive feeling. We were all a field of love. And in that field, there was absolutely nothing but a sense of completeness and at-home-ness and certainty that "all is right." There was not even a smidgen of anything "off" in it.

This dimension was beyond anything separate or trouble-some. There, everything was complete perfection and satis-faction. It felt more real than the realm of everyday living.

When I became aware of returning to the normal state of life, it was self-evident that this field of love is what we always are, despite our appearance in the ordinary world. I remember thinking—just as I was again aware of the world of separateness—"Oh, mommy's wrong," because I knew that everything was actually love.

My mother, despite her caring and lovingness, would (without realizing it) sometimes transmit a message of anxi-ety about life, but I knew then that there was no reason to be afraid. I intuited much in those moments. I remember very clearly having a sense of knowing that this Completeness is who we really are and that this place is most likely where we go when we die. Perhaps we don't stay there permanently, but it is a place where we go to rest, and that is our real home. Being very young, I didn't have many words, but I sensed that I could not share this knowledge, and didn't even try. This experience repeated itself later, and each time—when I came back to normal reality—I would recall the other times and put the experience away. It was not something I could talk about, and it didn't fit in with anything that was taught by my parents.

So I filed away this experience. Later on, I realized it was subtly driving me beneath the appearance of things all the time. I always knew there was more than what was shown, but I couldn't understand how to get to it. When I began reading spiritual literature in my young adulthood, I recognized that in India these experiences would be classified as yogic states of Samadhi (or absorption). But at the time, as a child, I had no words for it, and it was outside of the shared reality for somebody growing up in a New York housing project.

When I was in elementary school, I would think about it every once in a while, asking myself, "What was that?" I felt that I knew a secret; because nobody was talking about this, and there was no way I could explain it to my parents.

At some level, this experience was continually working on me, and nothing that was on offer in the world that I saw was satisfying. I longed for more meaning than what I saw around me, and this led to many years of spiritual exploration using whatever means were available.

Spurred on by a desire to get to the heart of things, I immersed myself in various spiritual paths, benefiting much from each one—even if I also found limits in them as well.

Where I Went with It

As a boy of 14, I looked for what was on hand to quench my spiritual thirst in the 1970's New Jersey neighborhood into which we had moved. So, I gave myself to a personal relationship with Jesus Christ and a strict form of evangelical Christianity despite my parents being nominal, lapsed Catholics.

Later on, in my late teens, I became involved in eclectic eastern new age spirituality and experimental lifestyles. By my mid 20's, I was meditating daily and working with a powerful teacher who was trained in psychotherapy and Buddhist meditation. I later became attracted to traditional forms of Buddhism, mainly Tibetan practices.

In 1992, almost by accident, I came across the teacher

HWL Poonja, who was one of the last living disciples of the great Indian sage Sri Ramana Maharshi. My times spent with Poonjaji were the most powerful and clarifying encounters I ever had. He was at once an intensely devout man in the Hindu Bhakti Devotional tradition as well as being a staunch proponent of non-dual Advaita Teachings. My experience of myself and the nature of reality was changed forever in the presence of Poonja. With him, there was an awakening recognition of Consciousness as being what I always already am.

After Poonja's passing, I found myself attracted to a community of spiritual teachers who were actively bringing non-dual teachings into a more relational, embodied, emotional and practical sphere. In association with what later became the Trillium Awakening community, I found myself developing in ways that I did not expect, with my identity as an all-pervading energetic presence awakened into a transformed life. I then became a teacher and spiritual counselor as part of an alliance of like-minded teachers, assisting people in awakened living.

We Are Each a Unique Tapestry of Being

Over time, my own view and way of teaching developed. Central to this approach is the notion that the world's traditions are our common heritage and are resources for us, regardless of which of them we find ourselves more (or less) committed to. With this foundation, it then puts your own experience front and center.

The traditions focus on perfecting specific potentials in life. I see our evolution moving toward being able to skillfully make use of all that came before us to bring forward new amalgams of transformation while appreciating and respecting the ancient sources. From this perspective, in the end, it is our own path that we walk, and all teaching is pointing to our unique situation and contribution. You weave it yourself, and your tapestry will be different from anyone else's.

The Tapestry approach shows how to make use of the many different techniques, perspectives, and practices that are available in such a way that they deepen a singular unfolding process rather than cluttering it. At the same time, it avoids the trap of chasing certainty and allows you to open to new possibilities and ways of thinking when you are ready to. It helps you to keep your balance in the face of the unknown. I don't know if this way of using spiritual paradigms is new. Sacred teachings employed as a means of orientation to mysteries rather than as a set of answers to mysteries may indeed be ancient, but few people have related to the traditions that way.

It seems to me that the belief that one can treat any particular system of thought or way of life as the total answer is not a very useful one. The idea that it is possible to have the instructions to life that remove the mystery (and danger) from it is not believable anymore, nor does it seem desirable. So the notion of guidance takes on a new significance today as many people consider themselves to be outside of any particular tradition, and "spiritual but not religious." They don't identify with being under the authority or control of any organized group with claims to have "the" truth.

The Tapestry is an orientation for individual free souls. Whether we function as part of a group or on our own, it is in a spirit of freedom. In a sense, the Tapestry lays out an almost universal orientation for spiritual living. It's generic in its description but is always a unique and individual brand as each person lives it. The distinctiveness of our own expression and revelation is central to this understanding.

As an orientation, it faces you toward your life in such a way that you have a sense of moving forward with spiritual progress happening through you, much more than that you are "doing it." It is also just as much about sinking more deeply into each moment now—savoring the quality of Being, itself—in such a way that you can see beyond the concept of time.

So life unfolds as a spiral path where you find yourself going through the same spaces you were in before, but differently. So it's not a strictly linear process. At the same time, you will not feel you are just going around in circles, but instead, you will be aware of how you've changed. In this case, the next "level" is the form your existence takes when you give yourself to where you are now, experiencing it as an increasing wholeness. You don't avoid one state to cling to another; you embrace whatever state you find yourself in, in such a way that it naturally moves you into the next.

One cannot know much about another's progress. Our next level can be a deeper version of the one we just left behind, but no one else may see that. This journey "around the Mandala," or through the Tapestry, uncovers your union with everything through the various nodes of experience. In this way, we use the Tapestry Mandala to help us as we weave our own personal Tapestry of Being.

As we move along our unique exploration through the nodes of experience, it is all founded in Consciousness Itself. I describe Consciousness Itself as being both embedded in life, and also beyond all possible experience. Our life is discovered as an ornament and a manifestation of that which never changes.

Our appreciation for all we live, both the highs and the lows, becomes a natural form of worship. Experience is seen both through the shared lens of objectivity and the secret intimate lens of Radical Subjectivity. Being reveals something exclusive to you, in particular. Your life is a living conversation describing a private revelation never known to another soul. You discover yourself as a singular juncture of countless threads; a precious yet transitory expression that gracefully points to that which is beyond experience.

There's a Way in Which ...

Imagine that we're in a room full of ancient sages, the founders and masters of all the spiritual traditions and the lineages associated with them. Imagine further that we have only a limited amount of time to be with them. In that situation, instead of wasting time trying to figure out who is "correct," my question to myself would be "how can I listen to them in such a way that I hear their message as they wished to convey it"? I'd want to suspend my own position—at least for the time being—to understand them. So, to help serve this purpose, I started using the phrase, "There's a way in which."

When a tradition says; "This is what is," I allow myself to see the way in which it is true, without having to decide it is the only truth. This simple understanding opened up everything for me concerning the verb "to be." With it, I can hear the person, and the tradition, speak what they want to say. I get the value of each speaker's truth because they are experts in what it's like to proceed from that assumption, and there's much that I can learn from each perspective. Each perspective was or is a living spiritual tradition, so there is a way in which it is a reality in the sense of being the lived experience of another person, as well as a sustainable truth for a whole mass of humanity.

I strive to take this approach with each view presented by these various traditions, and this way of holding things produces in me a unique perspective in itself. It may appear to be naïve, but there is more here than meets the eye.

Letting Perspectives Have You

Part of the Tapestry approach is to allow yourself to take in different perspectives without having to believe that any particular point of view is THE teaching that explains everything.

I think we will always have preferences that we are more comfortable with—that's natural. The question is how to (at least temporarily) set that preference aside and take in a new perspective while still holding our own truth. Can we allow ourselves to give ourselves the benefits, contributions, and gifts that these other ways of seeing may have for us?

A great many contradictory teachings are available today. How do you make good use of all these pieces of genius when so many seem to beg us to take sides? Unless we are willing to take the perspective of a particular teaching from its own side, then we are not in a position to understand what it is trying to convey to us whenever it says anything.

From the outside of a particular teaching, we only end up agreeing or disagreeing—that is to say, we are either "for" or "against" the statements or tenets of that teaching. In the Tapestry approach, this debate becomes beside the point because we want the flexibility of allowing in the benefits of more than one view.

While each node of the Tapestry Mandala can be the basis of a path in itself, each node also contributes to our capacity to live creatively in the other nodes as well. I hope that, by the end of this book, you will have a deeper sense of how each node of your life contributes to the others so that you can embrace any part of your life in a way that nurtures the rest of yourself as well. The Tapestry Mandala will help you orient on your quest. In it, there are three nodes of identity and three corresponding nodes of relationship. It is a simple picture of inclusive non-duality. Chapter 1 will give an overview of the Mandala itself, and the rest of the book will go into greater detail about each node.

Chapter 1
The Tapestry Mandala

The Tapestry Mandala is a visual representation of spiritual life with each "node" on the tapestry being an area of awakened living. It sometimes happens that one part of our life is developed in isolation from, or in direct opposition to, other parts of ourselves. An example would be a reliance on our identity as Consciousness to the exclusion of human relationships. Some spiritual paths subtly encourage this, even when they don't realize that's what they are doing. However, the suggestions here come from the Tapestry's inclusive, integrative view of spirituality.

Every node is distinct from every other node, but the Tapestry Mandala contains a spectrum of colors to convey the sense of continuity, showing how one dimension of the spiritual life is related to another and how they flow into each other. Also, within each node, there are shades of the next colored node on the spectrum because the distinction between the nodes is gradual and seamless. In the history of humanity, there have even been fields of study that focus on the particular shades of each color. However, I will not be making anything like a thorough listing of all that, but rather I will give the gist of each of the six stations on the Mandala with its colors on the spectrum and a description of how you can use this approach in your life.

Here are the six nodes of the Mandala:

1. Transcendental Divine Identity
2. Energetic Presence Identity
3. Embodied Human Identity
4. Embodied Human Relationship
5. Energetic Presence Relationship
6. Transcendental Divine Relationship

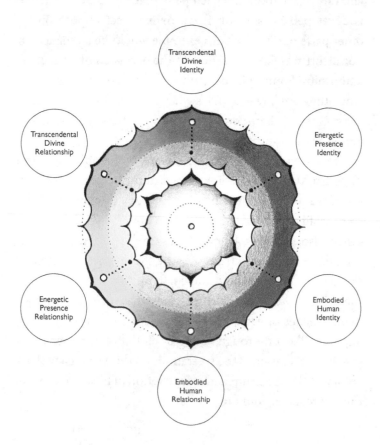

A Process: Awakening, Embodiment, and Fire

Along with the Mandala itself, there is a particular metaphysical picture that we will explore throughout the book.

From this view, at our foundation, we are Unchanging Awareness, the Ground of Being. At the same time, each one of us also appears as an individual sentient being—a moving, changing, embodied person living in a world that seems separate from us filled with other seemingly separate beings.

The primary form of spiritual awakening that we're pointing to here is insight and recognition into our nature as this unchanging awareness. When we awaken, we see that we have always been free from every appearance. Resting in this freedom, we may become aware of the current of feeling referred to as Shakti, energy, bliss or grace. If we are attentive to this dimension of vibration, feeling deeply into it, an integrating sense of authenticity can begin to inform our lives.

There is also the possibility to embody more of this energy and for it to overflow into a felt sense of non-separateness and one-ness with all of our experience. With this expansion, we can feel our individual sense of I-am-ness become a current that pervades all experience.

It may be helpful to remember that this feeling of connectedness does not come exclusively with the sensation of pleasurable bliss. Our process will blossom only if we are willing to meet whatever uncomfortable feelings there also may be.

As we embody more of this energy over time, the habits of the body and mind that we developed from the perspective of separateness are challenged and exposed to our now non-separate sense of experience. Rather than being buffered from the feelings that arise, we are now non-separate, yet open and available to whatever is happening inside.

The "vertical dimension" is the Consciousness that transcends personal identity, and is the context in which this transformation happens. The Transcendental Divine Identity is always already the case, without seeking or horizon. It is the baseline or the ground of everything, and in itself, it does not have any content, yet it is filled with potency for manifestation that comes forward and becomes the life lived. But in and of itself it is the formless ground of Unconditioned Awareness, untouched and unaffected by any transient phenomena.

The "horizontal dimension" is this process of your life unfolding as the embodiment of a flow of ever-changing energy and states. It is an emphatically unique and personal process. You are embodying the energies of the universe and expanding your sense of identity. Yours is a unique Tapestry of Being. You have a special song to sing, and whether grand or humble, you are here to play a part that no one else can.

What's more is that there is no singular "you" to be, you are a continuously unfolding mystery, not a static object; in that sense this process is trans-personal. As we continue the awakened life, we see that different situations and people bring inherent qualities to fruition; the world of relationships reveals more of who we are. There is a direction to the process coming from inside you toward fuller authentic expression, and the universe appears to conspire with you in this. Who you become continues to surprise you and is ever beyond the person you previously took yourself to be. Your devotion to the Intelligence and Love that orchestrates your sojourn calls you home.

This process can be both humbling and empowering and requires compassion. You find that you are more fully present with the immensity of life, with its awful horror and stunning beauty. It is not a straightforward process of immediate expansion, but rather an often-difficult heroic odyssey of expansion and contraction. Three steps forward and two steps backward. It is not a final destination of perfection, but an endless call to integrity through trust and surrender.

The Nodes

12 o'clock position / Red
Transcendental Divine Identity
You Are Freedom Itself

Here you explore an ever-deepening recognition and claiming of your nature as Consciousness Itself. At the 12:00 position, the top node of the Mandala, there is that aspect of the spiritual life that is the realization of our Timeless Nature.

This has been given many names, but it is ultimately beyond description:

- Unbounded Awareness
- The Self
- Consciousness Itself
- Spacious Awareness
- Buddha Nature
- Christ Consciousness
- The Conscious Principle
- Nature of Mind
- Intrinsic Awareness
- Unconditioned Awareness

Red is the node of spiritual awakening into our nature as the principle of Consciousness Itself, our Transcendental Divine

Identity, our Conscious nature as emptiness or formless Awareness.

Consciousness Itself is never an object that is known, but is rather the underlying context and awareness of everything that arises within it. It never changes and is without apparent attributes. It is simply Consciousness that is aware of change and objects.

Just as there are many shades of the color red, so there are many shades or types of teaching having to do with this node of life. All the teachings of non-duality point to this Red area, the essence of which are direct teachings on Pure Awareness.

Examples of traditions that specifically focus on this node are the schools of Zen, Advaita Vedanta, Dzogchen, and Mahamudra. Other schools may provide instructions about this node but they don't put it at the center of their emphasis as these schools do. We are speaking here of what a school emphasizes. For instance, Zen emphasizes the Red node, and while it also offers guidance concerning the other nodes as well, the Red node is its raison d'etre.

Some teachings border on two nodes: for example, non-dual schools of devotion bridge Red and Orange.

Some non-dual schools also include and emphasize teachings on the Radiance of Being, Shakti, Bliss or Presence as a door from the Purple node into the Red node. Those would be Maroon.

2 o'clock position / Purple
Energetic Presence Identity
You Are a Multidimensional Field of Radiant Energy

At the 2:00 position, the second node of the Mandala, there is that aspect of the spiritual life that is the experience of our nature as Radiant Being. This is your Energetic Presence Identity, where you are radiance and vibration. In the Purple position, we are exploring the field of being and current of feeling that flows through (and ultimately is) you and all that you experience.

As we move into Purple, we are speaking about the Energy of Consciousness rather than Consciousness Itself. There are specific forms of spiritual awakening within this realm, although the Energy of Consciousness is different from Consciousness Itself. The Purple node pertains to the field of radiant energy or vibration that comes into manifestation and is the substance of all that we experience, while Consciousness Itself is never an actual object of awareness.

In the Purple node, awakening is to our nature as Bliss, Presence or Shakti. These are perceptible and are ways of speaking about the natural power that emanates from Unconditioned Awareness or Consciousness Itself. This energy and peace are inseparable from unmanifest Consciousness Itself but they are perceptible and can be experienced and felt. This field of homogeneous energy is Purple as it emerges from Red. It is still a kind of non-duality, in that it is felt as one's self even though it is something experienced.

As we move through purple into shades that are closer to Blue such as Indigo, we are embodying energy instead of being it. The energy there shows up as particular meridians, channels, chakras, and auras, which are part of us rather than being us.

You could say that in its most expanded state, Energetic Presence Identity is the partner of Transcendental Divine Identity (Red). There's radiance of Consciousness, a field of energy. Depending on the particular tradition, it's explained as being either inseparable from the Transcendental Divine Identity or as the very first emanation or manifestation of Transcendental Divine Identity. Your nature as Consciousness—you as un-findable being—directly radiates a presence, an energy. There are all sorts of practices that can assist you in contacting that radiance or presence and help you maintain your connection with it.

The Taoist tradition is full of teachings about cultivating one's energy, recognizing it as part of the flow that moves (and is) all things.

There are practices in Hinduism having to do with Shakti-pat or receiving of the transmission of energy and the awakening of Kundalini. In many tantric schools, you may do things to amplify the transmission so that you enliven your field of radiance, your sense of yourself as an all-pervading energy. But it should be understood that in the context of this node we're talking about this radiant presence as your identity rather than as an "other" or a deity.

4 o'clock position / Blue
Embodied Human Identity
Discovering the Dignity of Your Divinely Human Nature

Embracing our humanity, we meet the vulnerability at the heart of our life, and we contact the finiteness of our mortality. It includes our personality, and our soul as well as our particular flesh and blood body-mind. It is about living in the subject/object world as the individual center of our lives. Here, we establish boundaries, acknowledge needs and desires and own the limited nature of our lives.

The Blue node comprises our traits, tastes, body type, ethnicity, and gender. This node also includes delight in the senses, the arts and the earth itself. Those aspects of our humanity that are possible only in relation to others begin to move us into the Teal zone as we approach the Green node and Relationship itself.

In the Blue of Embodied Human Identity, the energy of the Purple node becomes further solidified. The Tapestry Mandala is a spectrum where the nodes are not discreet sections but rather exist on a continuum and where the energetic field of Purple becomes the forms that are you in the Blue node.

Regarding the body, in the shades of Blue that are close to Purple, there is energetic anatomy. Things like Chakra systems and chi meridians are on a spectrum from "more subtle" to "less subtle" layers of Embodied Human Identity with both of them being maps of subtle energies. Finally, we have the human body of biology and chemistry.

Blue is about particularity. It is the entire human affair with all its frailness. In the Tapestry this is all part of the spiritual life, and we risk falling into the trap of "spiritual bypassing" if we ignore it. When we say "embodiment," we mean that we are embodying all three of our dimensions of identity: Consciousness, radiance and the personal. So this is also not merely identification with limits. It's about being a human being and feeling your human-ness, limits, and incapacities, but in the midst of an awakened life.

The Tapestry of Being is an inclusive form of non-duality. It's a both/and view. It's not that "I am not Consciousness Itself because I am human," and it's not that "I am not human because I am Consciousness Itself."

Teachings that use the view of exclusive non-duality are a brilliant skillful means to initiate us into a dimension of life that we would otherwise not be able to see, but the totality of life includes all its appearances as well.

I am Consciousness Itself, and I am also this field of energy, and I am also the human appearance as well. In my identity as the mortal person, I appear to be filled with limitation, I am always finding some way in which I am falling short, and life is always revealing the way it is limited. Embracing all of that is part of the awakened life as well. It includes both the pain and joy of existence.

6 o'clock position / Green
Embodied Human Relationship
The Catalytic Magic of Awakened Relationships

Green is the dimension of awakened relating where the multiplicity of the distinct otherness of every human (and every other embodied being) is honored and respected. In relationships, appropriate ways of expression and letting in the truth of others is a continual challenge. Interacting with others in mutual sensitivity as we recognize both our unity and our uniqueness creates a safe container for transformation.

The Green node of embodied human relationship further reveals what began in the Blue node. There are certain aspects of what it is to be a person that come forward only in relationships. Where the Blue node becomes Green, there is Teal; those are qualities where you're developing your Embodied Human Identity through being in relationships.

The world of others is the whole world of multiplicity.

You will see on the Mandala that Embodied Human

Relationship is on the opposite side from Transcendental Divine Identity, and that makes sense. From the perspective of Transcendental Divine Identity, or Consciousness Itself, there is no multiplicity. Your Identity in the Red node contains everything that appears in it, so there are no "others." If we consider the Red node as the formless place from which all reality manifests, then you can see each of the other nodes as an emanation of what was un-manifest in Red.

So, on the opposite side of the Mandala, you have "others" in all their multiplicity: Embodied Human Relationship. This is a kind of expression of the potency that is inherent in Un-manifest Emptiness.

There is unlimited possibility to manifest forms, to be all things. Each one of us is experiencing a unique combination of possibilities, and that's what we are; that's what our lives are. There's an unpacking of all the potential that's dormant in the Transcendental Divine Identity, and that ends up being the world of others and multiplicity.

If you talk to practitioners of the paths of Transcendental Divine Identity, they will often say things like "there is no other." However, if you talk to people who focus on Embodied Human Relationship, they'll say that this is a world filled with others, and that how we know who we are is through others. Paradoxically, there is a way in which both views are true.

Even as we are conscious of our boundaries and differences, we also become aware of the field of energies that connect us. We become sensitive to each person's own unique energetic nature as we move into the zones that are Chartreuse and approach the Yellow node.

8 o'clock position / Yellow
Energetic Presence Relationship
Unseen Help: Becoming Sensitive to Numinous Presences

This is the node where we uncover and develop our capacity to know that we are never alone. Here, we reclaim our heritage as residents of a spiritual universe, becoming sensitive to the numinous, and able to contact unseen help.

This Yellow dimension is the node of our awareness of, and our relationship with, the presences of both incarnate and discarnate beings: angels, saints, masters, guides, buddhas, bodhisattvas, gods, goddesses, nature spirits and departed loved ones, as well as the spiritual or energetic presences of people who are alive now but who are not in our physical proximity.

In a spiritual gathering, there may be a feeling of presence with which we can commune. It also can be that you feel different presences while being outdoors in nature. Many cultures cultivated the idea of being in communion with the spirits of nature or the energies of particular places.

For many people who are in a guru/disciple relationship, the Energetic Presence Relationship can be a primary factor. When that is the case, you are in resonance with your guru, and their body may be almost secondary. You may relate to their energy or presence as much as to their physical being. Their vibration stirs your vibration. In doing this, you can develop your Energetic Presence Identity in the context of the relationship through this harmonic resonance.

In Sufism, receiving a form of grace or blessing is called Baraka. In the Eastern Orthodox Christian Hesychast teachings, there is an understanding that one becomes transfigured and deified through participation in God's uncreated energies.

Your Energetic Presence Identity becomes full through catalytic resonance in Energetic Presence Relationships. All of these nodes are happening simultaneously and affect each other. Although we explain them sequentially, they are continuously interacting, and not linear.

Energetic Presence Relationship can be active even in the most human of situations. People who are in love begin to feel this, as do many people in long-standing relationships of any kind. Many of us can feel when those close to us are in distress. We can be caught by surprise that we feel these connections in our lives. These connections are an intuition of further possibilities, and they can be the beginning of a deeper Energetic Presence Relationship if you bring attention to them.

We often begin to feel people's presence when we think of them, even though their physical body may be far away. When a loved one has just died, we may still feel them, and if we talk to them, we may even receive answers. There is a whole world of activity even when there seems to be nobody there.

For many people, this felt connection may fade. But if you stay with this felt connection and expand it, you may then have contact with a realm of dear souls, those who have passed on and are still close to you. This blends right into the devotional world where you're aware of the presence of beings that you have never met physically, but whom you consider to be divine or exalted.

If you cultivate awareness of these diverse Energetic Presence Relationships, you may begin to recognize all energy as something you can be in relationship to as if in one single relationship. In the Hindu schools, this is the Goddess: The Energy or Power of God.

This leads us into the realms of worship and devotional traditions. Yellow into Orange goes into Transcendental Divine
Relationship, and that is relationship with the All-Pervading:
The Being that is being everything. You begin to relate to the
energy of the universe as a single lover or beloved.

10 o'clock position / Orange
Transcendental Divine Relationship
Devotion: Your Unique Relationship with Your Unique Divine

The Orange node is your experience of God (or Goddess)
as you understand and experience that One in your life. This
is the realm of devotion to the Divine Person in the particular way they reveal themselves to you. All forms of prayer
and acknowledgement of synchronicities become reminders
that there is simply one Beloved with whom you are in a private dance. Here you open to and acknowledge the Source
of Guidance in your life that is always present and personal
to you.

Like human love, the ultimate relationship is about heart
and feeling communion. There are many different traditions
related to the node of Transcendental Divine Relationship.
Some mystical devotional paths emphasize the way in which
we are embedded in and dependent upon the Divine. We
are in the position of surrender. We become transformed by
the reception of grace. We become holy and even divinized
through participating in the energies of God.

So, while there's a way in which the Divine is never separate from us, there's also a way in which the Divine is simultaneously distinct from us. Devotion needs "two" in order
to feel the current of love, yet for non-dual devotion this is a
paradox.

In India, there are both approaches: Identifying with God and worshipping God. There are those who say that we are God, there are those who worship God, and there are those who do both. One of the phrases that's well known among Indian devotees is, "I don't want to be chocolate. I want to taste chocolate." In other words, you need to be separate from the Divine in order to love the Divine.

And yet, the more you love All-pervading Presence, the more you find yourself in communion with it, and the more the sense of separation disappears. It's an ecstatic merging with the Supreme Power. Devotional mystics often use a sexual metaphor when speaking of this merging where Orange turns into Red. Relationship with Divine Radiant Presence outshines and absorbs everything else: As we move beyond words, there is non-dual dissolution. At this point, it is the Coral zone, approaching the Red node of Transcendental Divine Identity.

Orienting toward Mystery

The limitations of any teaching become apparent when we take it as a complete and total explanation of the Mystery of Existence. We can fall into a similar trap if we just dismiss any teaching that seems partial. It's useful to "try on" the understanding of something even if at first glance it seems incomplete.

As mentioned before, the approach of "there's a way in which" opens us to listen and learn. It brings respect and dignity to all parties, and it's to our advantage to be able to receive benefits from all the different information available.

When we see from only one perspective, we limit Being's capacity to teach us. If we are willing to trust that we will learn something even when we go astray, then we can move forward and hone our discrimination as we go along.

For example, the traditions of Advaita Vedanta and Zen Buddhism teach that only Consciousness is real and that what appears to us as the world is a kind of illusion or mirage that only causes confusion if it is taken to be real. However, the Non-dual Hindu Tantra tradition teaches that both Consciousness and what appears to us as the world are both real, but that they are not usually seen or experienced by us as thoroughly as they could be.

The Tapestry approach is that while listening to a teaching such as Advaita Vedanta, we ask ourselves this: Can we grant that somewhere along the line, perhaps in a way that we might not appreciate yet, it might be valuable for me to have access to the way in which the world is an illusion? And with that, we listen.

With this trust and openness, you can make full use of non-duality teachings that say the universe is an illusion. It helps you to see fully, appreciate and benefit from the perspective that knows the way in which the universe IS an illusion.

When approaching those teachings, it is useful to simply be interested in experiencing what those teachers mean when they say it's an illusion, and to let the teaching have us. We can choose to take the attitude that we just want to have the experience that is being described. The phrase "There's a way in which" makes it possible for you to then turn around and use non-dual teachings that seem to say exactly the opposite— those, such as Hindu Tantra, that insist on the way in which the world is real, and approach them with the same openness.

You can take on both points of view without having to know which is "really" the highest truth.

When approaching those Tantric teachings, it is useful to simply be interested in experiencing what those teachings mean when they say Consciousness and Matter are non-separate or non-different. In that way, we're letting that particular teaching have us. You may find for yourself a nuance or aspect of the experience that makes sense of the apparent contradiction if you work this way.

Similarly, if I'm doing Blue node work like working with a psychotherapist, I'm working with the ordinary, consensus reality version of "me" showing up and being authentic. In this kind of situation, I'm not concerned about whether any of what I share conforms to the reality of the Red or Purple nodes. At such times, I'm not referring to life as an illusion or a paradox. I'm just presenting myself as a human person living from my relative subjectivity. In the Blue node, the world I see is the planet earth of shared relative objectivity—consensus reality—and I live in the way in which all of that is real.

Of course, our experience of any one node is often naturally affected by our degree of development in particular other nodes but you are not necessarily trying to "fit" anything from your experience of one node into another. And even if you do find yourself trying to figure such things out, that's not the main point from the perspective of the Tapestry.

The Tapestry is a way to orient to Mystery using both your own personal experience and the spiritual insights of the ages. The Tapestry is not about trying to figure out who's got the best, most complete system, and it's not itself another map of systems. The Tapestry is an orienting towards Mystery in Mystery.

Follow That Which Attracts You

When I introduced this teaching, I found there were people who could see in a new way how the practices they were already naturally drawn to were serving them. This teaching became a validation of their unique spiritual unfolding, and a means for them to understand what they could do to deepen their experience and confidence in their own inner guidance.

The sequence in which we enter into each node will be unique to each one of us. It also may be that a particular person may live their whole life in only a few of the nodes. That's perfectly fine.

Our process can be straightforward and unforced. We move into what we are attracted to, and we may simply specialize in a few of the nodes for most of our lives. Many of the spiritual giants in history who have made the largest contributions have been specialists who followed their passion by delving profoundly into just one or two areas. They were not necessarily "balanced" concerning these nodes. Buddha was not Rumi, and Rumi was not Buddha. Both of them specialized in their focus.

Of course, that does not mean that we cannot lean into and live all six nodes. We certainly can do so and we may indeed be drawn to do just that. Many of us will find ourselves moving around all the nodes of the Mandala quite naturally. If you find yourself thinking about what to do, the way I would suggest to do this is to follow that which attracts you.

We can use the Mandala in any way we wish, but the effect is very different when we are following our own spontaneous attraction rather than approaching it as a checklist of things to do.

For example, if we have a passion for contacting a spiritual guide, we might use the Tapestry Mandala, and find that our passion is the Yellow node: Energetic Presence Relationship. Never having previously thought of spiritual guidance in those terms, we might see a new value in developing further in the Purple node as well: Energetic Presence Identity. So while it didn't seem relevant to us personally, at first, we can now see how it will serve us. We are moved into other nodes when our life takes us there—as you are moved, you quite naturally weave your tapestry.

Simultaneous and Sequential

The Mandala is an image of paradox. All of these nodes are simultaneous; they are always happening right now. Each of us has our attention distributed in each of them differently at every moment of our lives. There is no specific order or balance that is the same for everyone.

If you look at the Mandala, you are the center, and all of the nodes are the aspects of your life. In that sense, you are all of them, all of the time. And yet our attention is in every node continuously.

So, the Mandala is not a developmental map that lays out which step to do next. You will move from one node to another and back again, doing your own dance, in your own way.

In this dance, even what we take as our identity and the laws of reality continue to change. Who we are is quite fluid, and distinctions between us and the environment can be different at different times. That changeability is particularly true regarding each of the Mandala nodes. Our sense of what and who we are, just as our understanding of reality, is different in each node.

The paradox of being both human and divine is only the

start. It is only the beginning. The Mandala is a way to begin to be able to talk about the further paradoxes down the line.

The Tapestry Mandala is a Means

We sometimes want to find the "true" model for everything. We may assume we need to find the actual big picture that explains it all. It's useful to have maps, they are great, but the Mandala is not a map. It's not an attempt to synthesize all the traditions together from some objective perspective. The distinction between the purpose of the Mandala and a map is that this is not about "looking at" different views but more like "looking as" or "looking from" them. It's looking from the interior of possible points of view rather than looking at them from outside.

At the beginning, the Mandala will often seem to be a map. But if you look closely, you'll see that we're talking about a way of orienting towards traditions, with that orienting being from inside, from within your own personal experience of the perspective. It's also not "not a synthesis," but when it is a synthesis, it will be your own synthesis, not mine or anyone else's. You are going to have your own unique integration. It's your tapestry but it's not a pre-made synthesis.

In a way, the Mandala is a meta-perspective. I am trying to speak about an orientation rather than a particular point of view. Initially, it will seem like a template, a tool given by someone else, but once you digest it and deeply engage with it, it will become your own. You're walking the territory, not looking at it. No one can describe the particular path that you will walk, and you are not meant to walk anyone else's path.

As I mentioned earlier, maps are great, and it's not a matter of either approach being right or wrong. There's clearly a value in both of them, but there is a distinction. It's about building the ability to both "look as" and "look through" different perceptual lenses and then develop what is personally revealed to you.

The Tapestry, itself, is something that you will weave, but that will not happen by merely looking at things and finding the right ingredients and then putting them together.

It's more about participating with the impulses of Being. The question is "Where is Being moving me"? Then you notice, "Oh, it's moving me in a Blue direction. This Blue teaching here, that looks useful" or "It's moving me in the Green direction. I want to explore these teachings about the Green dimension." The Tapestry perspective and exercises in this book can help you to get in touch with your own internal guidance.

It can assist you in cooperating with your organic intrinsic movement, where you feel life pulling you. It enhances your confidence in your unfolding perspective. It becomes your unique tapestry because you weave it through your own walk, your own dance. You get a sense of how your direct, immediate experience is on the spectrum. You can also see how you are similar to or different from other people.

So while this teaching is not a particular synthesis, you will develop your own, naturally. We find a unique voice through listening to others. Being exposed to different perspectives can affect how we understand reality without any effort on our part to "get it right." And as I mentioned before, that way of being with paradox without having to "know" develops another aspect which is, from this perspective, most important: Trust. But to really trust, we must first know who we are.

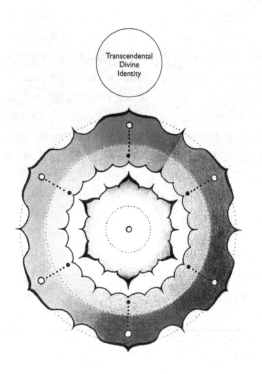

Chapter 2
You Are Freedom Itself

Red: Transcendental Divine Identity

There are many words used to point to the essence of the Red node, but depending on the tradition, those words sometimes sound like opposites. In Buddhism alone, there is "Big Mind," "Nature of Mind," and "No Mind." Language is not quite up to the task in this node—it can direct us to look, but can't quite grasp it and can even mislead us.

The Red node is about Awareness or Consciousness, but not consciousness in the way we use that word in everyday language. Here, Consciousness is Consciousness in Itself. It is the Awareness of experience, in which even our experience of being a human being is an object of that Awareness or Consciousness. It is the Subject of all our experience. Every sense field, every sensation, every feeling, every thought, is an object to that Subject. That Subject is you. But not the "you" that you have always taken yourself to be; rather, it is the "you" that is the Awareness of every sense you have of yourself. Our thoughts change, and our bodies change, but Consciousness Itself is unchanging and simply registers everything.

Just thinking about this doesn't change your life. For this to actually affect your life, it has to be seen directly. Self-inquiry is the practice of really looking for the Subject and examining for oneself what the nature of the Subject is. It is only in this way that we can go beyond a mere intellectual understanding. It is then the allowing of our attention to come to rest in the "position" of Consciousness Itself, that changes everything about the way we experience our world and ourselves. And that continues to be true whenever attention rests there.

Here the metaphor of a mirror and its reflections may be helpful. Just as a mirror allows every kind of appearance to arise in it; as Consciousness everything appears in us. The mirror is unaffected by all that arises, but the mirror never distances itself, removes itself, or turns away from what arises. There is nothing more intimate than a mirror and its reflections: they are one. Yet, even as they are one, the distinction remains; but as two sides of one coin, non-dual.

The most continuous, consistent and foundational aspect of what we are is not anything that we usually take ourselves to be. When we see for ourselves the absurdity of how we've been trained to live, we can't avoid coming to terms with it. We've been fearfully protecting what we cannot keep, while ignoring what we can never lose. It is tragic and funny at the same time.

Uncovering Our Unchanging Nature

The Transcendental Divine Identity is always already the case, without journey or horizon. Here you are freedom itself. It is the baseline or the ground of everything. In itself, it does not have any content, yet it is full with a potency of manifestation that comes forward and continually becomes the life lived. In itself, it is the formless Ground of Unconditioned Awareness, untouched and unaffected by any and all experiences or transient phenomena of any kind.

As mentioned in Chapter 1:

Here you explore an ever-deepening recognition and claiming of your nature as Consciousness Itself. At 12:00 on the clock, the top node of the Mandala, there is that aspect of the spiritual life that is the realization of our Timeless nature.

This has been given many names but it is ultimately beyond description.

- *Unbounded Awareness*
- *The Self*
- *Consciousness Itself*
- *Spacious Awareness*
- *Buddha Nature*
- *Christ Consciousness*
- *The Conscious Principle*
- *Nature of Mind*
- *Intrinsic Awareness*
- *Unconditioned Awareness*

There are many different names in the different traditions for this featureless Ground of Being and that can be a source of confusion unless you have directly experienced its nature for yourself. For instance, in some schools of Zen Buddhism, it is called "Mind," or "Big Mind." However, if you look carefully, you will see that they do not mean "mind" in the sense of thought, but rather the Space in which thought arises. In other schools of Zen, it may be called "no mind" or "mind without mind."

The important thing about all these names is what they are pointing to, not the label. The Zen master Hui-Neng said: "Truth has nothing to do with words. Truth can be likened to the bright moon in the sky. Words, in this case, can be likened to a finger. The finger can point to the moon's location. However the finger is not the moon. To look at the moon, it is necessary to gaze beyond the finger."

Red is the node of spiritual awakening into our nature as the Principle of Consciousness Itself, our Transcendental Divine Identity, our conscious nature as emptiness or formless Awareness.

Consciousness Itself is never an object that is known, but rather the underlying context and awareness of everything that arises within it. It never changes and is without apparent attributes. Consciousness is aware of everything including the usual sense of one's self.

Just as there are many shades of the color red, so there are many shades or types of teaching having to do with this node of life. Some teachings use the least amount of conceptual framework possible, while others use elaborate descriptions to make things easy to understand at first, but they then eventually coax you away from those concepts as well. *All the teachings of non-duality point to this Red area, the essence of which are direct teachings on Pure Awareness.*

Examples of traditions that specifically focus on this node are the schools of Zen, Advaita Vedanta, Dzogchen, and Mahamudra. Other schools may provide instructions about this node but don't put it at the center of their emphasis as these schools do. We are speaking here of what a school emphasizes. For instance, Zen emphasizes the Red node, and while it also offers guidance concerning the other nodes as well, the Red node is its raison d'etre.

The Orange Node Borders the Red Node

One can talk about Consciousness as the unknowable God, the Ground of Being, which contains all potential and yet is beyond everything. That's a legitimate way of describing the Transcendental Divine Identity from the perspective of the Orange node where the word "God" has that particular meaning in some schools of non-dual devotion.

There are saints of devotion, who are in love with the formless Absolute to the point of non-dual Identity. Kabir, Nanak, and Ravidas are examples from India and perhaps Rumi and Hafiz from Iran. When you read them, you sense that the One they are devoted to, and in love with, is both beyond them and yet is also their own deepest Identity. Their Beloved is beyond their small personal sense of themselves; when they surrender to that One, they lose themselves altogether as the small "I." That's an Orange node or devotional teaching blending into the Red node and would be in shades between Red and Orange like Vermilion.

The Purple Node Also Borders the Red Node

Some non-dual schools also include and emphasize teachings on the Radiance of Being, Shakti, Bliss or Presence as a door from the Purple node into The Red node. Those would be Maroon.

Although they are describing Consciousness Itself, they talk about bliss or a feeling of expansion, peace or grace as part of the description. This is because it is a major challenge to speak about Red without including some Purple in it. It is really almost impossible to say anything about Consciousness without also talking about qualities, even though Consciousness, in itself, doesn't have any qualities.

Because Consciousness doesn't have any qualities, you can't speak about it in and of itself. In fact, it's nearly impossible to talk about Consciousness without talking about it as if it were a spiritual object or state. Many of the descriptions of Consciousness, and the pointing out instructions, include words like spaciousness, openness, peace, and bliss. These are depictions that are taking in a little bit from the Purple node, including subtle objects of awareness (like peace or openness) to help us track and point beyond them into the Red node.

Consciousness is not ever an object of Awareness. Qualities such as peace, grace, bliss, and openness are objects of Awareness, they are not Awareness, itself. You often hear descriptions of Consciousness that include the word "radiance," which is using Purple node language to point to Red.

The Challenge of Speaking about It

And so, the tricky thing about this is that Consciousness Itself isn't an object, but there's often a subtle object or experience of some sort that is present within it when we look for it. But regardless of the beauty of any experience, it is still distinct from Consciousness, which is the Context of every experience.

Consciousness is present in every state. Getting clear about this is foundational in that it is the "You" that is continuously here, whether you're having a spiritual experience or a mundane experience. Consciousness Itself, is always present; your conscious nature is simply aware of whatever objects are there. It is our identity as freedom itself. The Red node is present in most spiritual and mystical traditions but different cultures relate to this Ground of Being in different ways.

Most of the traditions in the West tend to be on the Orange node side in relationship to the Ground of Being. Contemplative traditions in the three Abrahamic monotheistic religions—Judaism, Christianity and Islam—tend to contact, commune with and even merge with the Transcendental Divine through the language and perspective of devotional relationship.

In contrast to that approach, many of the traditions in the

East tend to be on the Purple node side. Meditative traditions in Buddhism, Hinduism and Taoism tend to contact, commune with and even merge with the Transcendental Divine through the language and perspective of our identity as Radiant Bliss and Peace. There have also always been unusual mystical traditions that have been inclusive of all the nodes.

Distinguishing between Red and Purple

There are many states that people identify as "Awakenings," so what this word means depends on the school. What is important in this context is to be able to see the difference between recognition of this Intrinsic Awareness and having experiences of states such as blissful energetic openings.

Many Indian traditions understand these states as forms of absorption or "Samadhi." One such state is called "Nirvakalpa Samadhi," a total or "No-Variety" state of absorption that is often pursued by yogis. When you enter Nirvakalpa, there is no sense of an experience or a person or any object of experience at all. In that state, the mind and all perception are totally absorbed in the Self, not in any way interacting with or cognizant of any outside world or experience. There is peace, but it is without any observer or experiencer, somewhat like deep sleep. Although Nirvakalpa Samadhi is a profound experience that is free of any multiplicity whatsoever, it isn't the most essential piece to focus on when studying the Red node because it is still a state. It is not what I am referring to when I speak about awakening.

Another type of absorption occurs when bliss or ecstasy outshines all experience as the Radiance of Being. It's known as "Bhava Samadhi" and is a profound non-conceptual state. The sense of separateness becomes absorbed into feelings of Power, Love or Awe. This outshining is a Purple node experience. It's about energy and radiance and can increase in intensity to the point where everything dissolves, sometimes giving way to total absorption.

It is not necessary to experience either of these two states in order to awaken to your nature as Intrinsic Awareness, but they can be very useful if they happen naturally, either before or after recognizing it. If these states do come, they can be extremely restful or blissful. Also, there can be a kind of deep reassurance about the reality of all of this that permeates you, and it becomes unquestionable after a while. But still, these are temporary states, they are not permanent; you have them and then you don't have them; they come and go, although a deep sense of certainty may remain.

The essential awakening to the Red node is the recognition that you are always the un-findable Awareness of every state and object. While the initial recognition is awakening to or realizing that your fundamental nature is this Intrinsic Awareness, that Awareness in itself is not the event of awakening. It is not a particular event, and it is not a particular state. It is present at every event and in every state, and it is aware in every node, not only in Red. Red is simply the node dedicated exclusively to Intrinsic Awareness in itself.

Every Moment is a Mix

This Mandala is a spectrum. It's a useful device to help you feel into what to cultivate and develop and to help you see where you are to some degree, but we are always experiencing more than one node at a time. Working with the Mandala is not a linear process.

Also, the Mandala is not a self-improvement program. It's

not a workout, as in "I have to do this node, and then I have to do that node." It's not that; it's more about following your own internal pull. It's about exploring where you feel drawn to, where you feel naturally led to do what you do. You continue to develop and see where it leads. It certainly isn't a purity test, like "I must be experiencing pure Red all the time."

The teachings that relate to the Red node such as Advaita Vedanta, Zen, Dzogchen or higher Mahamudra teachings, do not say that there isn't bliss; in fact, they speak about bliss quite a bit. So it's not that the Red node cannot have any sense of presence or any subtle objects of awareness. However, the main thing is to distinguish the Pure Awareness itself that is present in any moment, and doing this especially when you're aiming at clarifying recognition of that Unconditioned Awareness. It's about noticing what is aware of experience, not about whether there is Radiance or not.

Consciousness always has some object, that's the tricky thing about it, and why it's so easy to become confused about the distinction. Of course, it's especially pleasant when the object is a Purple node object, when there's a sense of radiance and bliss that goes along with the Pure Awareness.

What really matters is being able to distinguish Pure Awareness from any object it may be aware of. If you can distinguish that which is aware of this radiance when you're feeling it, then when you're not feeling particularly radiant, you'll still be able to recognize what is aware of the state that is there. Consciousness Itself is consistent in every one of the nodes and every state; it's always just registering what is.

Seeing beyond States

The Red node is the place on the Mandala where teachings on
Intrinsic Awareness reside. This node is where we focus specifically and exclusively on Intrinsic Awareness. Self-inquiry
is central to this. This is where you examine questions such
as: Where am I? Where is this "I"? Where is this awareness
of everything? Where is it located? We are looking for the
Subject, trying to find it. We are attempting to establish the
location of that which is aware of everything.

At first, on discovering that we can't find ourselves, we
may feel somewhat panicked, like "I am not getting it. I do
not understand this." It's a very typical situation with doing
Self-inquiry that "I just can't get it." At such times, simply relax and notice those thoughts and wonder, "What's aware of
those thoughts?" Keep on looking and noticing what is aware
of even that.

With persistent inquiry, there can be recognition that
indeed the Awareness of all experience is beyond anything
sensed, and yet is unmistakably You as the Subject.

In this pursuit, we feel a kind of bliss or spaciousness, an
expansive state that is a result of the act of looking, but it's a
side effect, kind of a fringe benefit. The purpose of inquiry is
not to have any particular state but instead to look to see if
you can find the Awareness of whatever state there is.

When you see that your conscious nature has silently been
registering all this, there is often a state that accompanies seeing it. I like to think that Intrinsic Awareness is like a woman,
a friend who enjoys having company.

Whenever anyone comes to see her, she dresses up in her
best clothes.

She wears peace, bliss, joy, and relaxation. Although it's

great that she throws a party when you look for her, the downside is that you might not recognize her if you see her in the supermarket wearing her sweat pants.

If we identify Consciousness with a particular feeling state, we can be confused when the feeling changes. It's like "Wow, that was great! I got the insight that I'm Spacious Awareness. It was so blissful, peaceful, expansive, but I don't feel that now, so I must have lost Awareness." However, that feeling of expansion, bliss, and openness, in itself, is not Consciousness. Consciousness is what's aware of all that. If we think that feeling state is Consciousness and if we believe that is what Consciousness looks like, then, when we're feeling angry, afraid, or our mind is racing, we'll say, "Well, I've lost it. Consciousness isn't here," but this belief reveals a misunderstanding.

What is aware of a mind that is racing? What's aware of anger? Consciousness Itself is. Whatever she's wearing, whether it's bliss or pain, she is always directly aware of whatever is happening. Consciousness is already there. Pain just indicates that attention has become fixated on some object. When attention is free of objects, there is a blissful feeling. Attention is a subtle form of mind. It is not the same thing as Intrinsic Awareness, which is always registering everything, yet by nature is never fixated on anything. When attention goes to look for its source, then these pleasurable side effects happen. As long as attention abides "there," there is bliss, and yet Consciousness always shines everywhere regardless of what attention does.

Our Points of View and Natural Samadhi

Once we know our nature as Red, unfolding further is about becoming used to simply being Awareness and noticing the mind that notices the mind.

For example, "I seem to have a point of view" is a great thing to notice. At such times, we simply notice what's aware of this point of view. Also, just notice the thoughts that arrive that say, "Well, maybe I shouldn't have a point of view" or "Is it enough that I have a point of view?" All those ideas are seen.

This is all just the mind being active, wondering about what it's seeing, while Unconditioned Awareness, Itself, is simply that which is aware and doesn't have any notion whatsoever about any of that. Any notion whatsoever is only another object of Awareness. Like a mirror and its reflection, the mirror is not concerned about reflections; they are whatever they are. There's always something arising, a point of view or whatever, but what arises does not define that within which it is arising.

When we begin to do self-inquiry, we may think, "I (insert name) am doing self-inquiry, so I can find out about what 'my consciousness' is." At first, that's the only way we can proceed. That is entirely understandable, and that's how we have to start. At some point, for many of us, this is seen to be a thought construct. The "me" or "I" that we take ourselves to be is seen to be a story that we tell ourselves. It then flips around, and it becomes evident that Consciousness has "me" arising in it. "I" (insert name) don't own a consciousness. Consciousness simply is, and the notion of "I" as a person, as well as everything that is experienced, are arising within Consciousness Itself. That includes the idea of any "I" as a person and a point of view. The idea of getting it and losing it is seen to be just more "thought stuff" within Intrinsic Awareness.

Any experienced state is simply more content within Intrinsic Awareness, even the outshining of existence in Bhava Samadhi or the empty state of Nirvakalpa Samadhi. Those states can be valuable, but what is more important is what is sometimes called "Sahaj Samadhi," the recognition that everything that's arising is arising in Unbounded Awareness itself and that you, yourself, are that Unbounded Awareness. Sahaj Samadhi simply means "natural Samadhi," the natural state. Some Zen folks have called it "Ordinary Awareness" because it's not an extraordinary state. Anything can arise within it—anger, pain, blissful pure lands, and heaven realms too—all the same.

Sahaj Samadhi also includes the tacit sense that whatever appears is itself a form of Consciousness Itself. Everything is arising in Consciousness, and everything is also a manifestation of it, not separate from it, so in that sense, it's all Consciousness. This is a key point.

Care must be taken here because we are on a razor's edge, and this is a place where some of the languages of particular non-dual traditions have differed. Consciousness Itself is unchanging and unmoving, and yet there is a way in which the changing experience that appears within it is not something other than it.

You as the perceiver may experience a shift and change as an "awakening," "seeing" or "realizing" of who you are. And yet, it's useful to consider that unchanging Consciousness has no need to awaken to itself because it's already self-aware. What awakens to Consciousness is the body/mind. When we distinguish between Consciousness and objects, this is what we recognize. And yet this will remain a subtle form of duality if we stop there and don't go beyond the appearance of separation.

This is a paradox because the truth of non-duality is that there is ultimately no multiplicity. All duality is a mere appearance, and in that sense, an illusion. And yet it appears. Depending upon how you define "reality," it is either real or unreal, but in any case, the situation is more than it appears to be.

Just as the appearance of objects on a video screen can appear to be an entire world of separate objects, but is actually the activity of the unmoving singular screen, so it is that all things are an appearance in Consciousness. This is the realization of non-duality regardless of what drama is on the screen of Consciousness, even if it is the drama of awakening. On the screen, if there is a dance of separateness and union, at the point of "union" the images can be seen as the dance of the screen, and in that sense there is only screen. Words are merely pointers here and if we cling to them, we appear to stumble. With this, we make distinctions for the sake of clarity, and then they fall away.

Conceptual Descriptions Are a Start

The way I've spoken about these teachings is seeing them as "biodegradable" in that they are intended to dissolve after use. We're not aiming at having a bunch of concepts in our minds to negotiate through life. Rather, these ideas may help us to get in touch with trusting our capacity to see directly. Insight, an innate wisdom that is self-generated, is the outcome. The Mandala is a means to an end. Any useful metaphysics isn't complete, and in that sense, no dharma or teaching is the whole truth. It's a story that we use to get deeply in touch with a profound sense of our own guidance.

From my perspective, the very nature of spiritual reality is intensely personal and individual. Even though conceptual categories are being used here, they are more about pointing you toward getting in touch with a kind of deep intuition within yourself so that you can trust what is next for you to do and explore.

It is not that I have a map of the Ultimate Reality and that I'm giving you some practices to follow so that you will then discover some ultimate truth that I know. It's more that, having been faced with a mystery, I found certain ways of orienting myself to it that have been deeply fulfilling and enriching for me. This orientation has helped me to get deeply in touch with a sense of inner guidance. So, the main purpose of Tapestry Teachings is to assist you in finding both the unchanging freedom that you always are as well as inspiration to open to all of life.

Transcendental Divine Identity Is Your Identity but Not "I"

This gets difficult regarding language. You are the whole Mandala in the sense that it describes you in Identity or you in Relationship in every node—it's all about you. However, you can exist without the sense of "I," and that is your identity in the Red node.

You certainly are Consciousness Itself, no doubt about that. In that sense, "You" are found in the Red node. It's just that the "you" that is in the Red node is not the "you" that you take yourself to be.

Your identity shows up differently in the different nodes; the way you show up in the Red node is as Consciousness Itself, but Consciousness Itself isn't the human person, it is that which is aware of the human person—and at the same time, it is the human person's true identity, in the ultimate sense.

Subtle in Its Power and Profundity, and Easily Undervalued

Understanding all this at the intellectual level is not enough. Real understanding needs real self-examination. A teacher can assist you with instructions that point out Intrinsic Awareness, but in the end, this must become a form of self-inquiry. Self-inquiry is something that you do with direct attention, not with thinking. Many people find this difficult because they become distracted by thoughts and feelings.

Even for those who have had a glimpse of this recognition, it is easy to miss its profundity and see it as just another experience rather than the bedrock of their spiritual life. Pure Subjectivity is not itself a state, nor is it something to attain, but the capacity to rest attention in the position of Consciousness once it is recognized varies from person to person.

If attention is addicted to thoughts and desires, then we may not give ourselves the luxury of relaxing into our essential nature. The real knowledge of the import of Consciousness is directly proportionate to attention's dissolving into it. Without spending time with attention basking in the direct knowing of this, we may wonder what is the big deal about Consciousness. However, no amount of explanation can convey it.

Guided Exercise

Here's an exercise that you might like to have someone read to you the first time you do it. There is a very basic way in which you are not the objects that you are aware of. This is easy enough to see when the objects are external to the body and mind but it can be tricky to see that we are not internal subtle objects, like our thoughts. The purpose of this exercise is to help distinguish the pure subjectivity of Awareness from the objects of Awareness.

Whenever you're ready, close your eyes and relax. Just notice the sensation of your breathing. You are aware of the sensation of your breathing, are you not? In that sense, the sensation of your breathing is an object to you. You are not it, you're aware of it. You're the subject. It's an object.

Now, notice the sensations of your body. Notice the way in which those sensations, taken together are an object to you as well. You're aware of them. You're aware of the sensations of your breath and you're aware of the sensations of your body too, are you not? In that sense, the sensations of the body and breath are not you. They are objects to you, you're aware of them.

Now, notice if you can feel the energy of your body. People report this differently. Some people can experience energy running through their body. Some people experience energy around their body. Some people don't experience any energy at all. However you experience it is ok. Just notice whatever energy there is. Include whatever energy you are feeling with the sensations of the body as well and just notice that the body with its energy is an object to you. You're aware of it. In that sense, you're the subject and it's the object.

If you're feeling any kind of transmission, or any kind of presence, any feeling that is more expanded than your body, or even the presence of the room itself, include that. Include all the sensations that you feel along with the sensations of your body. And include your breathing and just notice that all the sensations together are an object to you. In that sense, the whole field of sensation, the "kinesthetic field" or the "feeling sensation field," can be experienced as an object to you. You're aware of it and in that sense, it's not you, you are aware of it.

Now, notice the sounds in the room, whatever other sounds you hear. Sometimes folks hear high pitched noises that other people can't hear—you can include those too, whatever kind of internal static noises there are. Both external sounds and internal sounds—just notice the whole field of sound, the auditory field. It's also an object to you. You're aware of it, are you not? In that sense, it's not you; you're aware of all the sound. You're the subject; it's the object.

Now, whatever tastes there are in your mouth right now, allow yourself to become aware of those tastes. And whatever smells there are, allow yourself to become aware of those smells and just notice, you are the subject while tastes and smells are objects to you; the gustatory field and the olfactory field are objects to you.

You might see some light right now. If your eyes are closed, you can probably see little bits of light on the other side of your eyelids. Just notice the entire visual field, everything that you can see is an object to you. You're aware of the visual field, are you not? In that sense, this visual field is an object to you. You're aware of it. You're not the visual field either.

Now, notice whatever it is that you're feeling emotionally. It could be a neutral emotion, or curiosity or frustration or boredom or interest. Whatever emotion you're feeling, just notice what you're feeling. You're aware of it, are you not? In that sense it's an object to you, it isn't you. The emotional field keeps changing. You're the subject aware of the emotional field, and it is the object.

You may notice some thoughts arising, one after the other. Whether they are images, sounds or words, there probably is some kind of thinking. You're aware of thoughts, are you not? In that sense, thoughts are not you. You're the subject while the field of thought or "mind," is the object. You're aware of thoughts. You're not the thoughts.

Some people feel some sense of a "me." Some people feel this sense of "me" and some people don't. It's the sense of me-ness, a felt sense of your self. If you don't feel it, that's fine. If you do have the sense of "me," notice that you're aware of that too. In that sense, the sense of "me" is not you. You're aware of it so the sense of "me" is also an object to you and you're the subject, aware of it. So even your sense of "me" is not you.

As we've been doing this exercise, you have moved attention from one object to another. You are aware of this attention are you not? As subtle and close as it is, you are aware of it. In that sense, attention is not you. You're aware of it and so, attention is also an object to you, and you're the subject aware of it.

Also, throughout this exercise, I've asked, "You're aware of such and such, are you not?" and "in that sense you are not such and such." As that was said, there's been a kind of noticing in you, that's going "Mm-hmm" like a checker or a discriminator of sorts. This checker, this discriminating awareness, is comparing and checking "Mm-hmm. That's right. Uh-huh, that's right. Yeah, that's right." Notice that this discriminating awareness is making distinctions. You're aware of this discriminating, are you not? So, in that sense, the discriminator is not you because you are aware of it. You're the subject. It's the object. It's a very subtle object, but it's still an object, it's not the subject.

Now, see if you can get a sense of the subject. See if you can bring attention to the subject. Can you get a sense of it?

If you can't, that's fine.

If you can, then I am going to ask you, if you have a sense of it, what would you call it?

Let's call it "A" here, but you can use your own word for what your sense or experience of the subject is. If it's emptiness, if it's spaciousness or whatever you're experiencing, let's call it "A."

You're aware of "A," are you not? Well then, in that sense, "A" is an object to you, even if it's spaciousness, even if it's vastness; whatever it is, it's an object to you. You're aware of it. In that sense, "A" is not the subject. "A" is an object.

See if you can get a sense of what's aware of A.

If you can't, that's fine.

Now, let's say you do get a sense of what's aware of "A." If you do have a sense of what's aware, let's call it "B" here, but you name it whatever you sense it is or experience it to be. Now, Just notice that it's an object to you. Whatever that is. Whatever you have a sense of, you're aware of it, are you not? So if you have a sense of "B," you're aware of "B" and therefore "B" is an object to you; so it's not the subject, it's not you. See if you can be aware of the subject itself.

When you are ready, open your eyes.

Discrimination Finds Its Limit

What is it that you experience when you look to see what is aware of experience? Even space itself is a subtle object. There's a noticing that this looking for the subject could continue forever, isn't there? What is aware of this noticing that this could continue forever? Can you get a sense of that?

If you have a sense of it, whatever that would be would also be an object to you wouldn't it?

Here the discriminator or discriminating awareness is turned to the Subject. Discrimination is the aspect of the mind that's used with objects in the world to distinguish between different objects or between different aspects of an object. However, in this context, it's turned to face the Subject.

There is an infinite regress of the discriminating awareness, which hits its head on a glass ceiling of sorts. It can only go so far.

It's a bit like a miner wearing a helmet with a light on it. The miner cannot see the light, but he sees everything else by means of the light. Although the miner cannot directly see the light, he can realize or recognize that there is a light source on his head because he can see everything else.

Obviously, there is the Subject or Awareness. Throughout the entire exercise I've been asking if you were aware. You're the subject and it's the object. I've been talking about "you" being aware, but where is that "you"? "You" are never an object. This insight is not just a matter of belief but can be directly recognized or realized.

The discriminator can discriminate that something is aware of it, but it cannot directly experience that something. Discrimination knows that something is aware of the discrimination, but "it" (the subject) cannot be seen or even sensed directly. Only objects are sensed, and "it" is not an object.

Discriminating awareness notices that the Subject is aware of the discrimination but that it is not, itself, the discrimination. That's as far as the discrimination can go. The discriminator can discriminate that something is aware of it, but it cannot know or experience that something. So, Discriminating awareness finds that it, itself, is the limit.

You Are Not Findable

Obviously there's awareness of each of these objects—"you" are aware of all of these objects—but the "you" that's aware of all of these objects is never findable and is not even a subtle object; it is not any thing at all.

All the teaching which speaks about experiencing Consciousness is a metaphor; it is not literally true. You can recognize or realize that Consciousness or Awareness is you, the Subject, and you can realize or recognize that Consciousness is aware of experience, but you can't actually "know" or "experience" Consciousness Itself.

When attention turns to find out what's aware of everything, then what is realized is that it's not possible to sense

Consciousness as an object. Even if you felt a sense of infinity, that's still not Consciousness. Rather, that's the expansion, the side effect that happens when you look.

Throughout the exercise, I've been reminding you that you are the subject. Obviously, there's a "you" that's aware of experience, a subject that's aware of everything, but what that "you" is, what that subject is, is not knowable. It's not findable. It's not possible to identify it if you take the stance that you are separate from it. There is only recognizing that you are being it, and then in being it there is nothing to say.

It starts to become a kind of infinite regress if you try to use discrimination any further in the same way. Going back and forth between seeing this limit through discrimination and then letting go of the discrimination is very helpful. It lubricates the whole being. It has a huge effect on everything.

This is the mystery of being conscious; we are ultimately un-findable but obviously aware. The subject is un-findable because it is outside the field of the senses. Because of this it cannot be sensed, only realized. We already always are it. It's never actually experienced in itself. Yet it is who we are! It is the basis of our entire lived existence but it can never be touched! It's amazing that so few people ever check to see who's minding the store. Everyone walks around acting as though they know what they are, but no one checks.

Seeing this, we cannot even say whether the subject (you) exists or not. The category of "existing or not existing" doesn't even apply to what you are. All of the language about this is metaphoric, it cannot be spoken about directly; it is beyond language. We can't really say that the Subject is present, but here we are! Sri Ramana Maharshi used to say; "Will anyone doubt their own existence?" The Subject is obviously not absent, but it can't be found. Buddhists challenge themselves to find anything like an actual self.

This is why throughout sacred history, "The Subject" (or lack of one) has been referred to in so many contradictory ways. What is recognized has been called "Atman" or "The Self" (because it's the subject, our intrinsic nature). What is recognized has also been called "Anatman" or "No-self" (because it's not ever findable). We can't even say exactly that "it" is "there" or "not there" because only that which is in the field of the senses can be known to exist or not to exist.

Like light, Consciousness or Awareness cannot, itself, be seen but it illuminates all that is seen. We experience light only by seeing its reflection as the objects that it illuminates. This is the formless Light of Consciousness, your own deepest subjectivity; in this sense it is your own deepest Self.

Radical Subjectivity

Radical Subjectivity is the perspective that everything is arising in Consciousness, and that is the base and starting point of everything else.

Most of the ways we have learned to think and speak are from the position of relative reality. As I mentioned earlier, in relative reality I describe myself as coming on to the scene of a world that already existed before I was born. I learn about relative reality from other people's perspectives. My parents saw me being born and told me I was. I hear these facts from the outside and make sense of my life by imagining myself as others see and experience me. In my mind, I look at "myself" as if I were another person standing outside "looking at" myself.

However, from the Radically Subjective perspective, I was never "born." There was initially no clear difference between my self and that of which I was aware. I only remember gradually becoming aware of things and making sense of them. One of the primary ways that I made sense of things was taking on the relative position that others reported to me and imagining myself that way.

That is the relative subjective sense of myself, a self-image that I generated and identify with, and as this relative subjective self, I see the world outside of the body as a relative objective world.

For most folks, the perspective of Radical Subjectivity gets lost, ignored or discounted. This is the case, even though it is our most basic and effortless reality underneath the relative world that we learned about through concepts.

Both Radical and Relative Together

I'm not suggesting that we should be living without any relative frame of reference, not at all. What I am suggesting is that all relative frames of reference are part of what is unpacked from the infinite potential for manifestation that is latent in the Red node.

Red is the non-conceptual "emptiness" node. Radical Subjectivity is "naked" in the Red node. But when Radical Subjectivity is dressed up as each of the other nodes, it is still fully there in its nakedness, under (and in) the clothes of each of them.

So Radical Subjectivity underlies the perspective of the whole Mandala in the Tapestry of Being. It is the real ground of all of the nodes. So in this way of orienting to the mystery of life, the perspectives of relative reality are seen as features, aspects, or parts of Radical Subjectivity to be embraced.

While remembering the Radical Subjective perspective in

any moment, we are free to make use of any relative perspective that is useful. We can also notice that Consciousness is naturally intrinsic to each node.

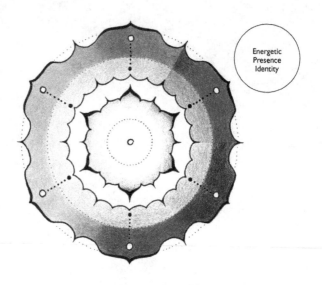

Energetic
Presence
Identity

Chapter 3
You Are a Multidimensional Field of Radiant Energy

Purple: Energetic Presence Identity

In this chapter, we'll investigate the sense of ourselves as subtle presence.

We'll broaden the context by looking at the importance of discriminating awareness in both the Red and Purple nodes and the difference between non-dual approaches that are primarily about "letting go" (renunciation) and non-dual approaches that are primarily about "transformation" (Tantra).

We'll start with a guided meditation that is similar to the exercise in the last chapter, but with a different emphasis. Again, as with many of the guided meditations in the book, you might want to have someone read it to you the first few times you do it.

Exercise 1

Whenever you're ready, close your eyes and relax. Just notice the sensations of your breathing. And notice the way in which your breath is an object to you, you are aware of it, you are the subject, and it is the object. Now, notice the sensations of your body. Notice the way in which those sensations are an object to you as well. You're aware of them. You're aware of the sensations of your breath, and you're aware of the sensations of your body too; you are the subject, and they are objects.

Now, notice whatever feeling sensations of energy are in the body, subtle sensations. Take your time. Maybe you feel energy running through the body or energy around your body.

Notice that whatever energy you feel is also an object to you. You are aware of the energy. You're aware of the sensations of the body. You're aware of the sensations of the breath. Now, if there's any sense of presence, any sense of presence at all, notice the way in which that sense of presence is an object to you.

Notice whatever sense you have of the presence of the room itself. Notice all these sensations together, the feeling-sensation field with whatever other sensations you are having. This field can be experienced as an object to you. You're aware of it.

Whatever you're feeling, whatever emotions you're having, just notice those as well and notice that those are an object to you. Sound, allow in all the sounds that are there and notice that you are aware of the sounds. Sounds, emotions, feelings, notice all of these together. They are objective to you. You are aware of them.

Also if you notice any smells or tastes, become aware of those as objects to you as well. If there is any light that you're noticing with your eyes closed, also include that as an object to you. Whatever thinking is going on right now, notice that is an object to you. If there is a feeling of "me" that you're aware of, include that as well.

Also notice that the whole time I've been speaking there's been a "noticer," a part of you that was checking, that's been able to see, "Okay, right, that's an object to me. That's an object to me. That's an object to me." It's a discriminating awareness, a kind of discriminator, that part of you that was noticing the differences; notice how that discriminator is also an object to you. Again, what is aware of this "discriminator," this "noticer"? If you have a sense of that "notice," that sense is an object too.

Finally, see if you can bring attention to the subject, that which is aware of all of this. Whatever sense of the subject you seem to have, notice that "sense of the subject" is not the subject, itself, but is also an object to you.

Give yourself time to just be.

Notice how everything is in you.

Now, just notice the breath again. See if you can embrace and merge with the breath with attention, allow yourself to become one with the sensation of the breath. Allow attention to merge with it. And those sensations of the body, see if you can allow your attention to merge with the sensations of the body so that you are the breath or the sensation of the breath and you are the sensations of the body.

Notice the energy that's surrounding the body or any transmission of presence, any sense of presence, any sense of energy that you feel. Allow your attention to merge with that energy, all the feeling-sensation that you're aware of. Just allow yourself to merge with that. Nothing to do, just be this feeling, all of this feeling.

Notice any emotions that are there, any feelings you have, whatever kind of emotions you have. See if you can just allow your attention to merge with whatever emotions you're feeling. Whatever sounds there are in the room, allow your attention to merge with the sound and become the sound. Allow that as well. Now even the visual field. Whatever you're seeing, just allow your attention to merge with the visual field.

Now, whatever thoughts you're noticing, just notice the thoughts as thoughts. Notice the space they take up, the weight of the thoughts. If you have a feeling-sense of the thought, just allow your attention to merge with the felt sense of that thought.

Whatever feeling there is of "me," the feeling of "me," that feeling of yourself when you say your name to yourself, that feeling, allow yourself to merge with that and include that as well. Now, when you're ready, open your eyes.

This exercise or guided meditation is an example of applying discriminating awareness, so you distinguish the way in which you are not the objects of which you are aware. And then, you also allow yourself (as attention) to experience the way in which you are everything of which you are conscious. That is an important aspect of the Purple node dimension. Because the whole Tapestry is a description of non-dual spirituality, you can find the experience of non-separateness throughout the entire Tapestry Mandala. However, the Purple node is particularly focused on this current because it's the node of the field of feeling-sensation, the energetic presence dimension.

You as the Field of Feeling-Sensation, Energy or Presence

Earlier we said:

At 2:00 on the clock—the second node of the Mandala— there is that aspect of the spiritual life that is the experience of our nature as Radiant Being. This is your Energetic Presence Identity, where you are radiance and vibration. In the Purple position, we are exploring the fields of being and current of feeling that flows through (and ultimately is) you and all that you experience.

As we move into Purple, we are speaking about the Energy of Consciousness rather than Consciousness Itself. There are specific forms of spiritual awakening within this realm, although the Energy of Consciousness is different from Consciousness Itself. The Purple node pertains to the field of radiant energy or vibration that comes into manifestation and is the substance of all that we experience while Consciousness Itself is never an actual object of Awareness.

If we consider this concerning the nature of Consciousness, then the Purple node is its inherent capacity for reflection rather than its invisible light (the Red node), but they are always inseparable. Pure radiance or presence is the first emanation of Consciousness. In the Indian non-dual teachings, the image for this inseparability is of Shiva/Shakti. Shiva is the emptiness or transcendent Consciousness while Shakti is the energy, potency or power that is radiating from Shiva. Depending on what language you use, and which school of thought you're in, this can be understood in different ways.

In the Purple node, awakening is to our nature as Bliss, Presence or Shakti.

The Sanskrit word "Shakti" means "power." But it's not merely impersonal juice, like electricity, because it is full of sentience. Empty Transcendent Consciousness radiates Shakti, which in itself comes forward as the primal energy of everything. It contains everything in potentiality that ends up manifesting as objects, including all sentient beings.

This is not to say that the Primal Energy of the universe is "a person" in the way we usually think of that word, but there is a way in which it is tremendously personal. It contains everything having to do with personhood. It contains all the qualities that we treasure in human beings like love, presence, and intelligence, everything that makes sentient beings valuable. And it is all of those qualities and more in a way that is totally beyond what we could imagine.

When I drive my car down the road, and I run over a pebble, I don't think about it. But if I run over a squirrel, it bothers me. If I run over a cat or dog, it bothers me even more; and it would be an absolute tragedy if I injured a human being with my car. Naturally, I place more value on a person than I do on a stone or a twig. The more personhood there is, the higher the value. It's possible when we hear that this is primal energy that radiates from Consciousness that we might think of it as less than human, as simply a force of nature. But this Shakti contains everything that is necessary to emanate and manifest everything and anything. It has all the qualities that are most precious. This point is something that's worth recognizing. This "Shakti" is often called "mother" because it is the mother of all life.

These are perceptible…

That is to say, you can feel and experience bliss, presence, Shakti or life force. In that sense, they're different from Consciousness Itself, which is not an object.

…the natural power that emanates from Unconditioned Awareness or Consciousness Itself.

This energy and peace are inseparable from unmanifest Consciousness Itself but are perceptible and can be experienced and felt. This field of homogeneous energy of the Purple node is a kind of non-duality. When you are in contact with this energy, you can experience yourself to be one with it, and you feel yourself expand and contract.

Our experience of energy or presence constantly changes. Sometimes it's experienced as a contraction and sometimes it's experienced as an expansion. In that sense, it's moving. It's changing. It's not like Consciousness Itself, that doesn't change. However, in the energetic field, there is still a kind of non-duality in it because we experience ourselves as non-separate from it, and this bliss of Being is beyond thought. You feel energy more powerfully when your attention is not engaged in thinking but is instead directly absorbed in the feeling sense. In that sense, it is non-conceptual, just as the recognition of Consciousness is.

When your attention is not on any object or thought, you rest only as Consciousness Itself. On the other hand, attention can be absorbed in a direct experience of the senses, aside from thought, and then you're resting in Shakti, the feeling-sense of Being or I-am-ness. This, too, is a non-conceptual experience.

To directly contact the experience of our senses without conceptual labels transforms the way we perceive life. Any experience of the senses directly apprehended without the thinking mind can be a doorway. For instance, when you place attention in direct feeling-sensation and ignore thoughts, then the feeling will draw your attention in such a way that there is no room for further thinking to have power to interrupt pure presence.

Even in physical exercise, energy tends to show itself as feeling-sensation when we ignore thinking that interprets (and interrupts) experience. Feeling moves you toward a non-conceptual state if you surrender attention into it directly. Probably the most common human example of this is during sex where there's an intensity of pure feeling-sensation. If attention is drawn into and merges with the feeling entirely, then you surrender to it, and there's no conceptual mind. It's just pure bliss, and release.

As we move through Purple into shades that are closer to Blue such as Indigo, we are embodying energy instead of being it. The energy there shows up as particular meridians, channels, chakras, and auras, which are part of us rather than being us.

There are many shades of Purple on the spectrum between the Red and Blue nodes. As you move toward the Blue node, you're moving into embodying energies that are both subtle and dense. On the boundary of Indigo, there are teachings that focus on energies moving in channels within the body.

Some of those teachings that are right on the border with the Blue node are about flowing energy for the sake of your physical and mental health. Right alongside and often mixed with them are teachings about tuning up your energy systems for the sake of awakening; they work with internal anatomy. There are various systems related to the subtle energy nerves known as "nadis" and "chakras" which are said to be centers or meeting areas of energy. Also, there are ways in which energy moving in channels can manifest certain ideal qualities and there are teachings that work toward that end.

There are teachings about contacting and drawing forth those attributes intentionally so that they come into manifestation in your energy field. They are abstract qualities that are felt in meditation and are then invoked into your energetic identity, so they become part of your presence. This is often done using mantras and mental images to draw down or call forth particular desired qualities into your energy field. All those teachings are within the Purple node.

When the energy is balanced and is flowing cleanly through these channels, it usually manifests ideal qualities effortlessly. When attention is resting in Consciousness, there's often an automatic radiance that contains love and compassion, kindness and peace. In that case, Purple is a natural byproduct, and the qualities are inherent to that.

In addition to these practices that bring forth or increase qualities or energies, there are also liberation teachings. They too are involved with energy, but the aim of those teachings is to release contracted or trapped energy into the whole field of Being where there's a sense of non-separateness and fullness. Those teachings are toward the Red node boundary.

There are two broad categories of teachings about energy anatomy: those that focus on attaining health and longevity, and others whose goal is the experience of awakening a current of non-separateness. These can all be applied as needed and they are all part of the Purple node as a whole.

Breath, Energy and Subtle Feeling-Sensation

There's a traditional understanding of the deep relationship between breath and spiritual energy so most energy systems include some kind of breathing exercises, such as Pranayama in India, Qigong in China, and Tsa Lung in Tibet.

There is direct access to changing the quality of your energy through your breath, and perhaps the easiest technique is to pay gentle attention to it. Without the use of an elaborate system, simply paying attention to the breath calms you effortlessly.

As a meditation object, the breath is perfect, because you carry it wherever you go. Whatever state you're in, wherever you find yourself, even when you're very disturbed, if you just sit and bring your attention to your breathing, your energy will change. Resting attention in the sensation of the breath and contacting feeling can be a deeply nurturing way to touch the flow of energy and presence that is always available to you.

EXERCISE 2

Here is a simple breathing meditation:

Close your eyes and bring your attention to breathing, just notice the sensation of your breathing, just as it is, nothing to change, nothing to do... Aware of the sensation of the breathing. See if you can allow your attention to sort of merge with the feeling sensation. Just breathing. Notice what you're feeling, whatever feeling you're having. Gently scan your body and notice. Find a place where there's any sort of comfortable presence or pleasurable feeling or emotion such as joy, peace, relaxation or warmth.

If you can't find any feeling that's comfortable, then do this with whatever feeling you're having even if it's a feeling that's neutral or not comfortable. Allow your attention to merge with the feeling itself so much that you, as attention, seem to become the feeling. Experience the feeling from the inside. Find yourself in the location of it, being it, spend a little time just being the feeling, without clinging to it or pushing it away. Simply be it.

Now, allow yourself to breathe into the feeling itself and relax into it as you breathe into it. As that feeling itself, allow yourself to become aware of the sensations of the rest of your body as well. Notice whatever bodily sensations are there, from the position of the feeling itself, as if you are the feeling being aware of the body. Now, breathing into the feeling, allow it to radiate and stretch out, and connect with whatever sensations you feel throughout your body as if the feeling were flowing into the whole body. Allow yourself as that feeling to become the whole body itself. Notice whatever changes in feeling there are as you simply rest here as the whole body itself.

When you're ready, open your eyes, and as you do this, notice whatever difference there is in how you feel.

Consciousness as Reflection Rather Than Light

We've been trying to put into language things that are difficult to describe. As an analogy for Consciousness, you can think of light; in itself, it is never seen. Even when we seem to see a ray of light, it's actually reflected off of little particles of dust, so we never see the light itself.

Although light is invisible, we know there is light because we see other things. When we see anything, what we see is light being reflected off of an object, that's how vision works. It's reflected light. We see light only when we see objects, and that's the only way in which we ever see light.

Similarly, we are aware of Consciousness only indirectly,

only in relation to objects. We are conscious of Consciousness, in a reflective way, through being aware of objects. As with the analogy of light, we never actually see Consciousness in itself. We become aware of it, we recognize it, but we don't experience it in and of itself.

Another analogy is that Consciousness is like a crystal ball—things appear in it, but the ball doesn't change, it maintains its clarity while things arise in it. A third traditional analogy is of Consciousness as a mirror—the reflections constantly change, but the mirror itself never changes. The mirror is profoundly intimate with its reflections, yet is entirely unaffected by any of them. Sometimes people speak of the unaffectedness of Consciousness Itself as if it's standing apart, detached, but that doesn't convey the way in which Consciousness is in everything, and everything is in Consciousness; there is no distance.

The Importance of Discrimination

It can be helpful to have a metaphysical picture in mind as a kind of context, and so we use a form of the traditional notion of the "great chain of being" in which Consciousness emanates Energy, and then Energy manifests solid or gross form. It can be a useful thought picture as a way to organize things in your mind, but there is no need to continually hold onto that as an image. It's not necessary to believe in it for the practical use of energy to work in your life. For some people, it intuitively makes sense. For others, it is a direct meditative experience—directly recognizing it without thinking; resting in it, in a state of contemplation. But you can still work with energy even without having experienced this picture. I will make use of it particularly in the three nodes of identity.

In this big picture, energy is always effortlessly radiating from Consciousness and is automatically self-liberating. There is also the far more common experience from a more dualistic perspective, in which a person's experience transforms from suffering to freedom. Even among those who have had an experience of effortless liberation, there is often a phasing in and out of it. In that case, discrimination is crucial.

In day-to-day life, what we experience is that we have a body, and are in that body. We are aware of the body, and we're aware of objects, and we have a feeling-sensation of being the body. From that standpoint, in practice, it comes down to learning to free energy and attention from patterns that we feel confine us. When this transformation happens, there is a visceral, immediate sense of feeling free, of feeling connected and spacious. You don't have to be in a higher non-dual Samadhi state experiencing an expanded energy field to benefit from that letting go.

By allowing yourself to release bound energy and attention, you have a fuller experience of all the rest of the Tapestry Mandala as well. You increase your capacity to become more present to what is, at any given moment. Here, discriminating awareness is key in freeing us from unnecessary suffering.

In the first exercise of this chapter, we gave attention to the "noticer" or a discriminator. It's the part of your mind that's checking things as in "Okay, I'm aware of sound and so sound is an object to me. I'm the subject who's aware of it." It's a kind of quick checking like "Uh-huh, I've got that, all right." But it doesn't think out a sentence like that, it's binary, and it's immediate. It compares. It just distinguishes one thing from another and it's always functioning very close to our experience of ourselves. It's the part of the mind that simply sees the difference between each and every thing in our experience. It simply notices a distinction rather than thinking about content.

The discriminator function is what sees a difference and it's also that which makes it possible to free energy and attention from stuck patterns.

It's crucial to develop that discriminating ability and to cultivate it but we can put it down like any other tool when it's completed its job. You want to be able to put it aside, but you also want to be able to pick it up again later, whenever it's needed. Without discrimination, you don't have the capacity to distinguish one thing from the other. It's a necessary, valuable tool.

Discrimination can also improve our concentration of attention. Our attention is often unconsciously and habitually hanging out in various places, but instead, at any moment you can ask yourself, "Where's my attention now?" Discrimination is our ally when it's developed.

For example, your friend begins talking about how she just lost five pounds. As you're listening to her talk, you hear the words "five pounds." Immediately, your attention quickly leaves your friend to rest on the thought "Oh, I wish I had lost five pounds!" and then your attention goes to the bloated feeling in your torso. Then your attention is on the image of you having eaten that ice cream today, and the next moment it's on the sad feeling in your heart area and the thoughts about how you failed to stick to your diet.

Then, when you come out of that for a moment, your attention goes back to your friend, and you're hearing her speak about how she wanted to take you out tonight. Suddenly you're saying "What? Oh!" You missed most of what she said because your attention was on the thought adventure of the many different ways you can feel bad about your weight.

From the moment at which your friend stated that she had just lost five pounds, that was it. However, if discrimination is keen, you can notice the thought that says, "Oh, I wish I had lost five pounds," and attention will not leave your friend. Instead, there is enough room to see the pull of your thoughts, and at the same time, you still have most of your attention on the living person speaking to you.

One reason people learn to meditate is to develop this kind of discrimination and concentration. That is to say, the ability to exercise choice about where to place your attention can happen only if there is a strong "noticer" or discriminating awareness. With this sense of choice, the outcome for the rest of your day can be drastically different. We can often choose to stop giving attention to negative thoughts or negative thinking without repressing or disassociating from them, by just noticing.

"Spiritual bypassing" is a term sometimes used for denying our uncomfortable or negative feelings in the name of being "awake" or "spiritual." However, for energetic transformation to occur, we instead need to be in touch with what we are actually feeling. We need to notice when we are rejecting what we feel, and that noticing is a form of discrimination in service of allowing us to feel what may be threatening or uncomfortable. There's no reason for us to feel shame or "unspiritual" in regards to any feelings that may arise. This bypassing can sometimes lead to a heady, split, dissociated, "disembodied" state in which we are always above it all. We have wings but no roots.

When people first discover the door to transcendent states or abiding as Awareness, they may cling to states of emptiness and no-self. This is the ego clinging to its "enlightenment." This is a common trap that we will eventually need to go beyond if we are to be whole. We can go beyond this by noticing if we are overriding or failing to see what we are feeling. However, there is also the other extreme in which we indulge the dance between thinking and feeling that exacerbates negative feelings and increases unnecessary suffering.

By choosing to place attention on more than your negative thoughts, you are not disassociating or being disembodied when exercising discrimination. When you clearly see that it no longer serves you to go back to the same thoughts that beat you up, you will just allow attention to see such thinking, feel such feelings and simply be present to them. That makes a huge difference, even if those thoughts continue to arise the same as they did before. In a very practical sense, that is an excellent use of discrimination.

Calm Abiding to Develop Discriminating Awareness

One way to strengthen discrimination is to use simple meditation practices with objects; spending time resting attention on an object and then seeing when attention leaves the object and gently bringing attention back.

The breath is a very convenient object, so it is often used. A mantra or a sacred word also work well. Or you can use a visual object like a flower or a statue or a picture. In each case, you bring your attention back to that object whenever you see that attention has wandered off. Doing this practice develops the capacity to notice.

One of the things that happens in meditation for most people is they feel that they're failing because they continually have to bring their attention back to their object. That's not failing. That's developing discrimination. If you had to bring it back only once, then you'd have only one moment in which you went, "Oh wait, there's a difference between thinking and resting attention on my object." That's what you want to develop, the capacity to notice that attention has wandered from the object. "Oh, my attention is on thinking." Just place the focus back on the mantra, or back on the breath.

If you notice 50 times in 20 minutes, then there were 50 times when you've become mindful, and you brought your attention back. The ability to bring your attention back is the capacity to notice distinctions—to see differences—and this noticing is the strengthening of that aspect of the mind (discrimination, noticing) which is so valuable.

We strengthen discrimination whenever we use a meditation object. That enhanced discrimination can be useful in many ways. One primary application is in recognizing Consciousness Itself. We distinguish between Awareness and everything else. Here we see that everything is an object to you and you notice "I'm not that, I'm not that, or that, or that." You notice that you're nothing that can be seen or known, and here you rest as you are. No location, no thought, no problem. That is the use of discrimination in service to the recognition of Consciousness, as in the Red node.

There are also ways in the Purple node, in which discrimination is used to distinguish between thought and feeling-sensation.

EXERCISE 3

Close your eyes. Notice if you're feeling any emotion right now. What emotion are you feeling?

Just see if you can allow your attention to merge with the feeling itself, with the emotion itself.

Whenever thoughts arise explaining what the emotion is about or explaining why you're feeling it, or even the name of it, see if you can ig-nore that for now, just ignore thought and allow attention to rest in the sensation of the emotion itself... Nothing to change... nowhere to go. Allowing yourself to be what you're feeling, to be the feeling-sensation itself. When you are ready, open your eyes.

Feeling-Sensation and Thought

The emotion may not change right away, but if you rest for a longer interval in the emotion, it often shifts and moves into another sense of feeling if you're not holding onto thoughts. The more you're able to simply allow emotion to be what it is without any labels, the more it will begin to move and change. Even if the emotion does not alter completely right away, it won't stay the same; our felt relationship to it shifts.

Often we are not feeling directly, but rather by way of thought, labeling what we're feeling, and we are not aware of that lack of discrimination.

Let's use sadness as an example: sometimes when we be-lieve that we are feeling sad, our attention starts in the initial feeling of sadness but then moves to thought about how or why "we're sad," and then we go back to feeling an amplified sense of sorrow. Attention weaves and dances between think-ing and feeling. We don't allow ourselves to feel our present emotion unmediated and directly. We feel a bit of sadness, then we think about why we're sad and then feel some more of sadness and think more about why we shouldn't feel sad-ness and then feel a bit more of that sadness. Back and forth. That's a complex that keeps feeling and attention stuck in a loop of exhaustion and pain.

A thinking-feeling complex keeps emotions locked in patterns. The more you're able to allow emotion or feeling just to be what it is and merge attention with it, the more you find you are no longer only with emotion but with an energetic presence, a sense of peace and deep feeling connectedness. Even sadness has a profoundly warm restful quality when freed from thought.

Exclusive Non-Dual Paths: Renouncing

There are paths of nonduality that emphasize the Red node almost exclusively. For example, the teachings of the modern Indian sage, Sri Ramana Maharshi, and the teachings of Advaita Vedanta that are related to him are very focused on the Red node.

Likewise, the teachings of Japanese Zen and Chinese Chan are forms of Buddhism that emphasize the empty nature of phenomenal existence and the unchanging Buddha nature. These teachings are about Consciousness Itself. They all use their own unique terms and have their own particular ways, but essentially, all the various Red node teachings are about attention resting in non-conceptuality or transcendence.

One interesting thing about these paths is that for the most part, they are founded or exemplified by people who come from a monastic orientation. Sri Shankara and the Buddha established monastic communities. Sri Ramana Maharshi left home life at 17 to live without possessions.

These are paths of renunciation. They are about finding transcendence and resting exclusively in that. They then counsel renouncing anything that may divert you from transcendence.

There's a whole spectrum in these paths of renunciation. On one end are those who entirely renounce the world, and on the other end are householders who live in the world but renounce living through thought, or at the very least they renounce the thought "I."

Ramana Maharshi is a good example of someone who was not concerned with anything other than resting in objectless Consciousness Itself. That path is to allow all the seeds of desire to dry up without giving them any attention, so all hope, fear, and sense of "I" dissolve of themselves.

You can spend every moment in vigilance with attention resting only in Consciousness Itself and not allowing a thought or an emotion to distract you. When attention is inevitably lost in some object or thought, you bring it back to the space of Intrinsic Awareness right away.

In this way, discrimination is exclusively in service to Consciousness Itself. You distinguish Consciousness from everything else until all desire for attention to rest anywhere else—on any object—falls away.

That foundational path is an excellent basis for clarifying the distinction between what changes and what is beyond change. But in its purest form it requires total renunciation. For complete success, you have to be at the point where there actually is no desire at all. It's very rare that people can pull that off directly. It's more likely that someone has an awakening to their Transcendent Nature followed by attention resting back on some sense of themself that is more limited. Very few people are ready to be free of all desire and the few who have been are like Olympic athletes, looked up to by everyone.

Many spiritual paths today come from this base of total renunciation but they modify it and work with the human condition to some extent because such a path is very demanding until you are completely ready for it.

Inclusive Non-Dual Paths: Transforming

Then there are non-dual paths that emphasize both the Red and Purple nodes together, such as Hindu and Buddhist Tantra. They are focused on transforming form as well as transcending form.

These paths also distinguish Consciousness from phenomena just as renunciation paths do. But while doing this, they also encourage engaging in life in such a way that attention contacts what is beneath the appearance of things: energy. In that way, the nature of desire changes because the nature of the world seems to change; it is experienced differently.

Consciousness is the unmoving space in which attention arises. Attention is not the same thing as Consciousness because attention moves around and can contract or expand. Attention is a subtle form of mind. By discriminating direct experience from labels or thoughts about the experience, attention contacts the experience of the senses directly. It is here that bare attention transforms the feeling of solidity into a nectarous blissful feeling quality. Here we can tune into fields of Energy and presence. Attention can merge with presence and energy in a way that is nourishing and freeing. This orientation allows attention to blend with experience and engages in life fully.

It is not necessary to renounce everything in order to proceed here, but discrimination is crucial. Discrimination in the Purple node is to distinguish between what we label within the sense fields as distinct from our direct experience of the sense fields in and of themselves.

There are many ways to cultivate the energetic presence dimension consciously and to discriminate between the juice of life and the thinking mind. For example, just sit and gaze into space in such a way that you relax your vision so that you are aware of interpenetrating shapes and colors; ignore every label that thought gives to this, allowing attention to merge with space. Or relax and listen to all sounds, both inner and outer, ignoring whatever labels your thinking mind presents to you. Get lost in the auditory field itself, merging with it all.

Though the cornerstone of transformation is to experience the energetic presence beyond labels directly, such paths often use secondary or auxiliary means of contacting presence. These are all to assist in the amplifying of energy, enhancing energy. There are many methods to do this, such as by using sound and mantras, by exercising the body in a way that opens channels, and by using visualization to open yourself to the presence of energy. There is a special method of doing Mantra in a vibratory fashion so that it can change your breathing and can massage internal energetic networks.

Energy is vibration. The use of sound, particularly mantra, can be used to enhance and explore the energetic dimension by chanting or singing out loud and by paying attention to the quality of your voice. You've probably noticed that at certain times your voice resonates more deeply than at other times. By noticing and paying attention to that resonance, you can get a sense of the chant or song's effect on your energy.

Also, visualization can be used to enhance or get in touch with a flow of energy or sense of presence. Here are a couple of examples:

EXERCISE 4

Relax and close your eyes.

Remember a time when you deeply experienced the life current, a sense of presence, or transmission, or when you felt your whole body full of energy. Perhaps it was as simple as the feeling of warmth while taking in a beautiful spring day. As you think of it and see it in your mind's eye, how do you feel?

Allow yourself to be filled with the feeling as you remember it, as if the experience were happening right now. Let the feeling increase. Commune with this feeling, allow it to saturate you.

When you're ready, open your eyes.

That's a very simple use of imagination to contact your sense of presence more fully. It's always there. We just need to bring our attention to it. Imagination or visualization does that very well.

Here's another easy way to amplify your feeling-sensation:

EXERCISE 5

Close your eyes. Imagine a sphere of rainbow colors in the center of your chest. If you can imagine it clearly that's great. If it's not easy to imagine it, then just feel the presence of your sphere of color. Feeling is the most important thing here.

Allow yourself to feel the presence of your sphere of rainbow color penetrating you like the warmth of the sun. If you wish, you could imagine this warmth as colored light radiating from your rainbow sphere shining in you like a sun, infusing the rest of you. Inhale with a feeling of reception in the heart. Feeding the radiance into the entire heart region, surrendering and relaxing and opening your entire body to your rainbow's transmission of radiance. Relax the mind whenever thoughts arise. Just ignore them. Simply allow attention to this process of heartfelt bodily reception of radiance. Breathe in the transmission of feeling deeply into your heart and on the exhalation let it permeate your entire body and all your energy.

Do this meditation until you are saturated and overflowing with feeling presence... It radiates out of you in all directions and opens up your attention too. Let in the space behind you as you continue to allow yourself to feel the sphere of color radiate. See and feel your sphere of color slowly turn into pure white light and dissolve. Stay with the feeling of this. When you're ready, open your eyes.

Just notice what you feel and allow yourself to feel it without description, simply being aware.

These practices tend to amplify the feeling-sense. Central to them is using discriminating awareness to distinguish feeling from thought. Often they employ images, sound or breath to contact presence but then you leave behind the tool and rest without thought in the current of feeling-sensation or Being-ness.

The Metaphysical Picture is about the Eternal Now, Not History

In one sense, the Red node—Transcendental Divine Identity—is the basis of everything. From it and in it proceeds the Purple node—Energetic Presence Identity—and then the Blue node.

The Red node is infinite, unknowable. Even beyond being or not being, it is indescribable. Within the Red node, there is infinite potentiality but no actual manifestation of that potentiality. It doesn't exist as any objective, experienced "thing," so there's a way in which it doesn't exist at all. Then that infinite potentiality comes forward as profound energetic power or presence like a great cloud of fullness and unconditioned feeling.

Here, energy is Shakti, power, fullness, unlimited feeling. It's filled with divine qualities. And there is an expansion like an unpacking of the potential. There are divine qualities, divine names, or archetypical currents like compassion, wisdom, and love. From there, forms arise that start out as energy patterns and then appear to be solid so there is the sense of a body and a world of objects and then we are here in the Blue node.

These are nodes of identity, and while they may seem to correlate to the stages of individual child development, this is not fundamentally a linear or causal description of things happening one after the other in time. It's more about what is the case simultaneously in each moment. Each thing depends on, or proceeds from, the other like a fountain in every instant. There's a relationship of one thing relying upon the other for its existence, but they are present simultaneously. In a sense, all of this is going on without beginning; it's always happening, even right now. It's a vertical depth, not a horizontal length.

The Red node is like the ground and the Purple node is the root, metaphorically speaking. The language is sequential for the sake of understanding, but that's not actually how it is. So this is not a teaching about how the universe came into existence during the big bang sometime in the past, it's about how our experience is coming into being now, right at this moment.

The more we develop our nature in the Purple node, the more everything in the other nodes is enriched, because the Purple node is the feeling root of our life.

There is an essential paradox in this notion of development because our experience of ourselves does not ever correspond to all that we are. There are two equally valid ways of seeing our situation in our Energetic Presence Identity. In one sense we are always expanding to become more than we are: enhancing, building up or further generating a spiritual body. In another sense, we are becoming ever more conscious of an energy body that is already the case and has always been here, but unfelt as ourselves, and in this life we will never come to the end of that expansion.

So this context includes that in some sense there is already radiance existing at the root of your being which is emanating the self that you are aware of consciously; and that radiance calls you home. It is that field of energy from which your gross body/mind comes, and it is that for which we long. It is the "fully expanded" version of ourselves that we unconsciously yearn to be or with which we long to merge.

There are two ways to see both the Transcendental Divine and the Energetic Presence. One is as Identity, which are the Red and Purple nodes, the other is as Relationship, which we'll look at more fully in the chapters on the Yellow and Orange nodes. If seen through the lens of relationship, this larger sense of yourself already exists right now and is drawing you toward itself, and wants you to embody all that it is, which is what you are. So there is a natural momentum in developing the Purple node such that we may find that life will cooperate with us and send us exactly what we need when we ask to open to it.

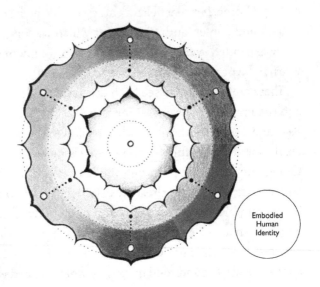

Embodied
Human
Identity

Chapter 4

Discovering the Dignity of Your Divinely Human Nature

Blue: Embodied Human Identity

It is not easy to be here. Bette Davis once said, "Old age ain't no place for sissies." I think that's true about life in general. We're heroes just for getting through each day. On the one side there are the demands that life seems to place upon us, while on the other side there's childhood conditioning and our struggle to go beyond all that so that we can live as free adults.

Many of us have a sense of being called to do something even if we don't know what our calling is or what value it will have. Much of the Blue node is about clarifying what is ours to do and what isn't. In the Blue node we need to be listening carefully to our truest sense of things.

Development of the Purple node helps with this listening because we can become more attuned to what we are feeling and to what we sense is calling us. The more we are attuned to our subtle preferences and feelings of satisfaction, the more we can use these as a way to focus our energy and attention. Then something meaningful can happen in our lives. Intentionally "tuning in" is something that changes the nature of even the simplest things.

Our actions are not a means to determine our existential value, but to express it. We can find ourselves in a flow of creativity using whatever work we do to focus our vision. We find ourselves as an artist of our life even if we may be doing something that appears unimportant. Then embodiment is an instrument of life itself.

Finding our sense of authenticity, learning to go beyond conditioned behavior and living from the impulses of being do not happen overnight. Patience with conditioned patterns must co-exist with increasing understanding and freedom as we unravel layer upon layer. From the Tapestry perspective, the truest uncovering of our human dimension includes all three nodes of identity informing our journey throughout life.

Bringing the Red and Purple nodes into our lives in a way that is ongoing and natural rather than only as exceptional peak experiences means we must embrace the most mundane and ordinary things as sacred. And that starts with bringing loving attention to our own body.

EXERCISE 1

Whenever you're ready, close your eyes and relax.

Softly balance your weight so that you feel grounded, allowing yourself to get comfortable. Breathe slowly and deeply so you can fully inhabit your body.

As you breathe, take a few seconds to become aware of how your body is affected by your breathing. Notice where your body is tight and where it is relaxed and expansive. Notice the weight of your body and where your sitting contacts it. Become aware of where there's a feeling of being supported, maybe against your back or under your buttocks or your feet, and notice the pull of gravity, allowing it to sink you further into your seat, into your chair.

Give yourself a soft focus on the surface of your body. Just become aware of the surface. Notice how the skin envelops all of your body. Allow yourself to be aware of the temperature, and your body's response to the temperature. Is it more tense or is it more relaxed than it usually is?

Now, gently squeeze the outsides of your arms. Notice the sensation. Squeeze your shoulders and legs, continuing to sense how that feels on the surface, on the outside, and on the inside of your body.

When you're through squeezing, take a moment to continue to notice what you're feeling. When you feel ready to stop, just take a breath. Register that small event. What was it like for you?

Be curious and see if you can allow yourself to feel a little more deeply into those senses. Take this moment to just relax with your body, your oldest friend and steady companion. Just acknowledge it with kindness.

Now, turn your attention inside. Focus on the sensations inside your body. Become aware of any places that feel particularly comfortable, and any places that don't feel as comfortable. No need to change anything. Just allow your attention to permeate what you're feeling. Allow yourself to feel your body.

Now, allow your attention to move around and explore inside. See if you can have a sense of the feeling of your organs, how they're all floating inside of you. Whatever sensations you feel; as if there is an anatomy chart, you're allowing yourself to feel the organs and bones.

Also, notice any flow of energy, breathing or any other sensation. Notice your heart beat. Simply notice. Nothing to change. Just be with this body. Just stay with this. If your mind wanders, that's natural, bring your attention back to the sensation of breathing. And as you relax, notice any sensations that are new.

Now, take your time and allow yourself to become aware of the larger sense of the room, gently allowing your attention to flow into the larger space around you. Open your eyes. Notice where you're sitting. Where are the objects in the room?

Divinely Human, Humanly Divine

In Chapter One we said:

Embracing our humanity, we meet the vulnerability at the heart of our life, and we contact the finiteness of our mortality. It includes our personality, and our soul as well as our particular flesh and blood body-mind. It is about living in the subject/object world as the individual center of our lives. Here, we establish boundaries, acknowledge needs and desires and own the limited nature of our lives.

The Blue node comprises our traits, tastes, body type, ethnicity, and gender. This node also includes delight in the senses, the arts and the earth itself. Those aspects of our humanity that are possible only in relation to others begin to move us into the Teal zone as we approach the Green node and Relationship itself.

This node seems to be, at first glance, the node that everyone is in automatically, innately, and in a sense, this is true. However, it's not possible to fully live our Embodied Human Identity without the other aspects of Identity also being part of our experience as well. To truly be present, it's essential to have access to our Transcendent and Radiant Natures.

The image of the Mandala is a spectrum with each color flowing into the next one rather than each node being discrete. It's like an old-fashioned analog clock rather than a digital one. So it isn't that our humanity is an entirely separate dimension, altogether different from the nodes on which it depends. There's a fundamental way that being fully human requires embodying more and more of the Purple and Red nodes as they seep into even the most common parts of our human life.

The Essential Vulnerability at the Heart of Life

One of the primary reasons we need access to our nature as Unconditioned Consciousness and Radiance is that for us as human animals, this planet is a really hard place to be.

From the time we were babies coming into the world, this existence has been overwhelming, and when we are open and undefended, it's more than we can handle as merely human beings.

As part of the normal process of development, parents condition their children in such a way that they become numb, or able to distract themselves and regulate their emotions to deal with it all. We cobble together a sense of ourselves that is at a distance from our experience, and therefore we are not entirely feeling or present to what is.

In terms of our human identity we are a body-mind. We can experience ourselves as a mind that has a body, or as a body that has an activity that is the mind, and both perspectives can also be balanced.

As bodies, we are profoundly vulnerable and as a way to help us cope with this situation, our parents, teachers and society at large condition us to experience ourselves as minds that live in bodies, rather than as bodies that have minds. This conditioning produces the feeling of distance and separateness from experience that makes things manageable. But we are only partially living.

So we are in the situation of feeling the desire to live more deeply, but are also afraid of what that might involve. We are living in avoidance of our essential vulnerability, and yet that vulnerability is the key to our authentic humanity. Letting ourselves drop into truly feeling where we are as mortals is a devastating proposition. If we stop distracting ourselves and let in the truth of the situation, it is a frightening picture. Everything and everyone we treasure is changing and dying. Nothing is truly dependable, and anything can happen at any time. It's a world in which one thing consumes another and nothing survives in the end. No wonder we won't allow ourselves to be completely here! We have a deep denial of death and that is actually necessary in order to function as a human being.

Fortunately, awakening to the Red and Purple nodes catalyzes another kind of awakening in the Blue node: an awakening to vulnerability at the heart of the human life. Realizing that I am not simply the body or the mind creates a new perspective when it is not a mere intellectual idea, but a direct realization. The exclusion schools of non-dual Awareness will often leave us permanently in the Red node, or in the Red and Purple nodes combined. These schools may counsel that it's enough to know you are transcendent and to maintain that identity exclusively—directly aware of, but not being, the body and mind. The language of exclusive non-duality often stops right there.

But inclusive non-dual teachings recognize that Consciousness Itself creates a safety net through which the manifest dimensions can be embraced when attention relaxes and drops into this precarious bodily life. As Awareness, we are always beyond the body and mind, so therefore, paradoxically, we can allow ourselves to be aware of the way in which we are also the body and mind as well.

Inquiry into Embodiment

First, we must awaken to Consciousness. That's the first step. Often people ask, "What is it that awakens to Consciousness?" As I've said in Chapter 2, it's useful to consider that Consciousness has no need to awaken to itself because it's already self-aware. What awakens to Consciousness is the body/mind. That is a key to embodiment.

Here's a three-step recipe of inquiry into embodiment. You can take as long as you need to do it, years even... but don't skip the order:

1. When ready ask: "What if I am that which is aware of all that arises?"

   Recognize yourself as pure Consciousness, inseparable from the infinite un-manifest Absolute. In other words, identify as Consciousness that is beyond the body/mind and all manifest existence, yet contains them. Notice that all that arises is arising in and as that Consciousness that you are.

Steep until ready.

2. When ready ask: "What if I am that which continues to arise?"

   Recognize yourself as that which arises as the limited body/mind, inseparable from the vast matrix of all manifest existence. In other words, identify as the body/mind, that which is both in Consciousness and yet a form of it. Notice that recognizing that pure Consciousness has always only been the experience of the limited body/mind and no one else.

Simmer until ready.

3. When ready ask: "What if I am both that which is aware of all that arises and that which continues to arise? And what if I favor neither identity but embrace them as if they were both true?"

Recognize yourself as both pure Consciousness, inseparable from the infinite un-manifest Absolute, as well as that which arises as the limited body/mind, inseparable from the vast matrix of all manifest existence.

Identify as Consciousness that is beyond the body/mind and all manifest existence, yet contains them.

Also, identify as the body/mind and all manifest existence, that which is both in Consciousness and yet are forms of it.

Notice that all that arises is arising in and as that Consciousness, but also notice that the experience of recognizing pure Consciousness has always been that of the limited body/mind.

This is a contradiction beyond logic, it is the paradox that we are. The effect of this recognition is to live within a sensitivity that is affected by life while founded in the space that is always unaffected. This new identification is more than recognizing the manifest life as a form of Consciousness; it is also recognizing that the experience of realizing Consciousness is something that takes place within the manifest life. It is not reducing life to a sub-category of Consciousness and it is also not reducing Consciousness to a sub-category of life. It is the embracing of both views being true, and this can be experienced both sequentially and simultaneously.

The result is to be dropped between the Source and its manifestation. This "gap" between Consciousness and phenomena is our fullest place of identification; here we are stretched to encompass all of our experience. Only in this gap can we be both, and honestly include all that we know ourselves to be, without dismissing anything. This gap is paradox itself.

Paradox and Simultaneity

Again, it is essential to see that you are always being more than one dimension. Initially, there will be a moving of attention and identification through the nodes, but by playing with the perspective that you are always more than one node at any time and by consciously allowing attention to rest in the realm of human limitation as well as in the transcendent, the different nodes are experienced more and more simultaneously.

Ironically, as both the unmoving indestructibility of the Red node and the wellbeing of the Purple node become established in the midst of our day-to-day human experience, we begin to feel the vulnerability at the heart of life as a sense of powerful authenticity. It's as if we now have a secure container in which we can allow ourselves to feel more of what previously we had been avoiding. This descent into everything about our human-ness that we had been wanting to escape from also transforms it.

The various attributes of our identity are then related to each other in an inclusive, holistic network. In this new context, various aspects of ourselves function differently than they did before. Even parts of ourselves that we didn't used to like may show themselves working in ways that we couldn't have anticipated. We become remade as we live from a more integrated foundation. This happens over time as we drop into the most basic of our human limits. A unified sense of realness becomes the direction of our lives.

Both Vertical and Horizontal

In both the Red and Purple dimensions there is a favoring of
the transcendent and non-conceptual. However, in this Blue
province, we add to that an affirmation of the body/mind
with all of its conceptual and emotional richness and all of
its messiness.

As we thaw out of the frozenness that had protected us
from our essential vulnerability into the wholeness of living,
we can find ourselves stretching to meet our challenges in apparently contradictory ways. There is the need to honor both
what we are in the present moment and also to honor our
natural impulse for more. If we collapse attention exclusively
into the desire for more, we will not be happy with or present
to what is. But if we ignore the impulse in us to go beyond
what is, we will not be happy then, either, because we will be
ignoring something that is arising in the present (the impulse
for more). This is related to the way in which we are always
"vertically" in the eternal now and yet are also developing
"horizontally" to reflect that "now" in manifest form.

The developing horizontal aspect of this is often gradual
and meandering. It is humbling because—if we are honest
with ourselves—we are well aware of the difference between
how we usually show up in our lives as compared with what
we know ourselves to be from the perspective of the Red and
Purple dimensions. However, we must always proceed from
where we are, despite wishing otherwise. Denial doesn't serve
us in this arena, although it may take time for us to discover
this for ourselves, sometimes repeatedly.

Our body/mind has been conditioned since childhood, or
even earlier, with emotional and behavioral patterns based on
assumptions of separateness. This is true whether you posit

one lifetime or countless incarnations. Even if those patterns seemingly disappear after awakening to our Divine nature, they often return. This is true for most of us, so if it happens to you, know that you are in good company. There is no need to either discount what you've realized or pretend that you have no patterns.

It is very fortunate that life habits and emotional patterns which are based in separateness do not have to be renounced outright because very few of us would be able to do it. Instead, we can work with them through a combination of:

1. Allowing them to be what they are while relaxing any resistance to them

and

2. Bringing discrimination to the assumptions on which these patterns are based.

Of course, this does not include behaviors that are immediately dangerous or life threatening to yourself or others; regarding those, you should do whatever is necessary to prevent harm. But for everything else, the combination of these two approaches will be a staple for the spiritual life.

If your idea of spiritual work or practice is to keep improving the horizontal dimension until it's perfect, that would be a recipe for suffering because the horizontal dimension is not ultimately perfectible. This work is not practiced in that way; it doesn't have an endpoint; its value is not a possession. This is instead a path of continuous deepening without thinking in terms of an end. The vertical dimension is always already perfect right now.

In the horizontal dimension, we are working with what is, even as we are allowing and meeting what is. Here, we are bringing to bear the "whole-being knowing" of the Red and Purple nodes to the conceptual, emotional and behavioral levels of life.

Allowing and Compassion

"Allowing" is to exercise intentional unconditional compassion toward all of our emotional life. Our emotions are real for us at that moment, even when they are reactive. Part of the difficult work in this node is to allow ourselves to feel without judging ourselves. This does not mean that we encourage or condone acting out, not at all. In fact, it is more likely that we will not act out if we allow ourselves to consciously feel our uncomfortable emotions. It is also more likely that we will be able to allow ourselves to consciously feel our unpleasant emotions if we have compassion for ourselves.

Rather than holding a model that requires us to have perfect feelings, we hold a perspective in which we meet emotions with acceptance, allowing attention to relax into and feel deeply whatever arises. That includes the feelings of non-acceptance, doubt, judgment, guilt, regret, and remorse. Meeting them with an open space of compassion and gentle affection, considering and reminding ourselves that we are doing the best we can.

This allowing of feeling is similar to what we do in the Red and Purple nodes but with an added emphasis. The space of Red is directly aware of what is arising and in that sense is allowing it. In the Purple node, the freeing of energy and attention that brings wellbeing comes through feeling without thought. Here in the Blue node we add intentionality and ways of thinking that support what we know to be helpful. This is the skillful use of emotion and mind to serve and support the insights of the Red and Purple dimensions. In this way, you are a firm advocate for yourself, even with all your human frailties, imperfections, limitations, and mistakes. On this foundation, too, we find we can begin to extend this same compassion to more and more other people we come to meet over time.

Discrimination of Assumptions and Thought

There is a difference between discrimination in service to non-conceptual Consciousness and presence, and discrimination in service to useful or skillful thought. In the previous chapter, we looked at how we can use discriminating awareness to free energy and attention from the feeling-thinking complex that keeps emotions remaining in patterns. Here, we add to that the capacity to think differently.

The finesse that is needed to discriminate in service to skillful thought includes a couple of important caveats. First, when we work directly with thinking, it is best to do so with things we have already actually experienced. It's not helpful to do this trying to convince ourselves about things we do not actually know. At the very least, the ideas should be ones that you trust and that you are experimenting with and willing to "try on." Also, we should not do this as a way to override what we are actually feeling. There is a sweet spot here where we are embracing and feeling what is arising as we also question what we are thinking.

There is a way in which all thought is always limited, partial and incomplete. But the Blue node is not an "all or nothing" dimension. There is relative value in relative reality, so not all thoughts and actions are equally valuable. This fact is understood throughout the spiritual traditions.

The truth of non-duality does not mean that there is no value in making distinctions within the realm of the relative. Non-dual Buddhism and Hinduism are quite clear about this, as are the panentheistic schools of Sufism, Stoicism, and Neo-platonism. All of these schools have some form of training the mind in order to think in terms that are supportive of our greater spiritual process. Part of this training is the use of conceptual reminders, slogans or phrases in addition to going beyond concepts.

By systematically applying what we know from our experience in the Red and Purple nodes to our habits of thought, we slowly change the way we think, feel and behave over time. We can usually do this much more consistently if we are already using exercises for developing discriminating awareness.

We have already explored ways to go beyond our thinking and have experienced what life is beyond the merely human dimension. Here we apply the recognition of the nature of reality that we have garnered from our direct experience of those other nodes to our thinking about everyday living.

To some degree this is effortless, but habits of activity based on the sense of fear and separateness are persistent. The skill is allowing and understanding emotions based on the assumption of separation from the Whole of Being, while also questioning and looking more deeply into them with insight. It is a continuous practice.

Being aware of the stream of thoughts and images that we have throughout the day and noticing which ones are simply impressions and memories of what we know to be true and which ones are manufactured exaggerations, distortions or generalizations becomes an essential inquiry.

This means we are aligning and unifying our sense of what we feel we can factually know objectively with the way that we represent things to ourselves subjectively when we think. We do this even as we acknowledge the limits of our objective sense of things.

So therefore, we work with the way we think about things and strive to think as objectively as we can about what we know, without adding anything. Just asking yourself the question "Is that really true?" can often do the trick. Clearing out the images and thoughts we have that keep us unnecessarily triggered and reactive can make a huge difference in our lives.

Another way to use thought to begin to affect our behavior is to intentionally bring to mind the bigger picture in which all of us are connected. We are part of the whole, and everything is part of us, as we can see from the perspective of the other nodes. We are one in Consciousness and are manifestations of the same power, so we remind ourselves to treat others with respect and dignity. Fairness and justice make natural sense because we are all part of the same human family, not only in the flesh but also in Being Itself. It can be helpful to have simple phrases that we repeat to ourselves to remember that we are all part of one whole. In that way, we support ourselves in living in alignment with that truth.

The ancient Stoics understood that—as individuals—our preferences are to have good health, wealth and a good reputation, especially among our friends, and that these things are naturally the concerns of our life. However, the vulnerability at the heart of life makes it clear that these things are neither a safe refuge nor an entirely manageable measure of our lives. While it is reasonable that we should pursue these three, they are ultimately beyond our control in every moment. Real

happiness lies in living authentically as a particular manifestation of the whole, as we naturally follow our desire to be
happy; it's helpful to remember that.

We cannot control what happens, but we can work with
our thinking about what happens. Accepting what is, whatever the outcome of events may be, is a virtue that is its own
reward. As we allow ourselves to rest in what is, we are always
at home wherever we are, because we have aligned our thinking with reality. We don't actually know how things should
be, and they are as they are. This is the challenge of surrender.

Here the serenity prayer of the American theologian
Reinhold Niebuhr comes to mind:

> *God, give me grace to accept with serenity*
> *the things that cannot be changed,*
> *Courage to change the things*
> *which should be changed,*
> *and the Wisdom to distinguish*
> *the one from the other.*

A few years ago, I was telling a friend that I had bought the
wrong tickets for some travel I was doing that ended up adding hours to my trip. His reply was "You're probably better
off; you weren't supposed to be on that flight." I asked him to
explain. "Well, the way I see it is that you can go through life
thinking you are the victim of things that didn't go your way,
or you can go through life thinking that the Universe has been
looking out for you, arranging things for your ultimate good.
Neither one is provable, and I choose to believe the latter."

Changing our thinking about what happens to us can reveal just how much investment we actually still have in thinking that we are merely and entirely separate beings in a hostile

world. However, we cannot rush any of this change in thinking and we need to respect every part of ourselves. When it comes to the horizontal dimension of life, some parts of us are still just getting on board.

Embodying the Energies of Being, One Step at a Time

If I think of myself as a thousand-legged caterpillar in a race, then in a certain sense, the race is over when the first legs cross the finish line. However, in another sense, there are whole parts of me that have yet to cross the line. Whether we think of the finish line as "Awakening as Consciousness" or "embracing embodiment" or any other mature stage of the process, this analogy seems to apply. There are parts of ourselves at various stages of this process at all times, and I expect that we will probably die before the last legs go over the finish line. But really, the race is already always won right now, and even more so as each leg goes over.

From my perspective, the human life is not about any final victory regarding health, wealth or even being loved. It's fundamentally a lost cause at that level even if we have great success in all those ways because impermanence and death will sooner or later have us all. In that sense, human life is about sacrifice to the whole from which we come, in which we live and to which we will return. There are beauty and profundity in every act of sacrifice because it reflects our function of existing for the whole. We are happiest when we serve something larger than ourselves. Remembering the context in which we are here to incarnate a particular display of Divine potentiality can give us a sense of meaning, however our lives unfold.

Our Unique Aloneness

In this context, the individual soul's nature is such that we are always aware from a particular perspective. What is essential to our humanity is our own uniqueness. We see things only through our own eyes. We hear things only through our own ears. The exclusivity of our experience is always ongoing but easily missed because we share this world with others, and we tend to forget ourselves in our shared world. So we already are individuals and that distinctiveness is a double-edged sword because it is also our sense of being alone and not understood.

That aloneness speaks to our inherent dignity and value. We're holding a piece of reality that no one else holds. If there were two or three other people in the room with us, even if all of us were looking at the same thing, we'd all be seeing it differently. Each person's experience is a particular angle that no one else will ever have. Even if we were all great meditators and could rid our mind of all thought, we'd still all be aware of the objects in the room differently from each other.

The unique perspective from the point of view that you experience within Consciousness is the foundation of your individual identity. This point of view is not Consciousness or the body-mind. If you are in an altered state having a vision in which you don't seem to have a human body, or if you have a dream in which you seem to be someone else, you have a point of view regardless of what particular body you have. So while the soul, or point of view, can be connected to a body, it is not confined to a particular one.

Many ideas have been posited about what continues after death. However, we are not focusing on that subject here but rather on the simple fact of having a sense of one's own existence that is completely unavailable to others. It's about the unique point of view, the unique perspective that each soul has, or is. That very fact is a unique value that each person has. You are seeing things that nobody else has ever seen or ever will see. In that way, you hold a unique perspective and value. Our very existence as a soul is to be alone.

Unity Is Simultaneous with Diversity

Consciousness radiates a conscious energy field. That conscious energy then becomes the human experience of bodies and objects, but this all happens in such a way that depletes neither Consciousness nor the energy. They, along with the bodies and objects, are still there, like a fountain always flowing from its source. It's an expansion or an unpacking of the potential, which leaves the Red and Purple nodes remaining as Red and Purple nodes even as they emanate into becoming the Blue node.

Vibration in Stillness

If you look at the earth from the perspective of outer space, you see that the oceans don't move. They're not going anywhere and yet there is movement within the sea. The currents in the sea are its power.

It's interesting. In some schools of Hindu Tantra, there is the notion that while Consciousness in its nature as space doesn't move, there is still movement within Consciousness. It is a "throb" or "vibration." That is the nature of the energy, the Purple node.

The ocean as a whole is not moving anywhere but the currents of movement within it are its power and that's the Purple node. That movement forms waves, and that's the Blue node. In its movement, Consciousness is not depleted nor any less when emanating the field of energy. It loses nothing, just as the currents and waves do not exhaust the ocean. The waves are a momentary expansion of the ocean.

Our human forms are momentary expansions of the energy of Consciousness. We are individual waves, and when we look at all the other waves, we don't feel so alone. There are many other waves, and they are all talking to each other in order to keep from looking at the beach. If they were to look at the beach, they would see what happens to the waves when they reach it, and it doesn't look very good. Life as a wave always comes to the same conclusion.

Those waves up ahead seem to disappear, and everybody knows that when the waves reach the shore, they won't exist anymore. But, if you're lucky, there may be a wave close to you that tells you "You know what? We're more than just waves." Such words would be only attempts at consoling philosophy if that wave didn't also tell us how we could find out the truth for ourselves. "Don't just take my word for it. I will show you what you should do to see for yourself. Dive down deep within yourself under the surface of the water. Bring your attention way down and look around down there."

So you, as a wave, dive deep inside, deep under the surface. When you go beneath the surface, you look around and see the vast sea, and then you come back up. Then, the other wave says, "See, that's what we are. We are the ocean." And that changes everything. And nothing. As a wave, you're still going to hit the beach, but the wave is the activity of the currents of the deep. Waves do disappear and become part of the sea, but they were never really anything other than that all along, so if they know what they are, they can never be lost.

The Interacting Nodes of Identity

In both the Purple and Blue nodes, there's an experience of different sorts of relative subject and objects.

In the Purple node, the relative subject and objects that appear are felt to be one and there is a current of non-separateness running through it all.

In the Blue node, a sense of limitation and separateness arise, and the feeling that we are only the body/mind can be our experience. Unless some of the Purple node shines through, it's as though the waves are experienced only as their surfaces.

The Red node is the place of the ocean depths where there are no waves of which to speak. In the Red node, non-duality means that we are nothing in particular and there is no identity of being a relative subjectivity living in a relative objectivity. There is no doer, activity has no individual actor at all and everything is seen to be happening of itself. This spontaneous appearance arises in you, but is not your activity, because you are not doing anything. If we go even further still, there is no one that could ever act, and nothing ever really happened.

From the Purple node perspective, it can be experienced that all the action that you're aware of is yours. You are being everything and doing everything but of course, it's not you as the relative subject who does that, it's you as the Radiant Power of Consciousness.

If you are simply being the space of the Red node, then you are doing nothing. If you are the Radiant Power of the Purple node you are doing everything. But when there is attention in both the Red and Purple nodes of Identity simultaneously, you are at the same time being the unmoving space and the Feeling of Being that is everything. Then you are being all of it and none of it at once—not doing anything at all and at the same time, being the spontaneous doer (dancer) of the universe.

In the Blue node we are the local, relative, sense of ourselves. If this relative sense of yourself expands beyond itself, so that it begins to be experienced as the energy in everything, then your sense of yourself is no longer limited to a single point but is felt to be merged with everything. You are the doer of it all. From this perspective, many people say they are God. It's the Subjectivity of the All.

All action seems to proceed from one place which is you, and which is also everyone because you don't feel any distinction between you and anybody else.

Many people have had the experience of suddenly recognizing that whatever thoughts they have or whatever knowledge they have, is coming to them from some mysterious source.

Sometimes the relative sense of "I" drops away, so that all information and knowledge—whether it is coming from someone else's mouth, or it is arising in your own mind—is clearly coming from the same source, because it's as if the other person who is speaking is speaking your thoughts... and you feel it that way. You're in a non-separate state such that all knowing is your own knowing. But it's not exclusively yours because in that state, you're not separate from the other person. There's a sense of union, not only with them but with everything.

This is also true of the sense of yourself as no longer being locatable in a particular place. You feel all-pervasive. You don't experience yourself as a relative subject in a relative objective world. There may be your body and objects and all that goes with them, but they are experienced in a singular Radical Subjectivity.

If we were in that state of simply Red/Purple nodes exclusively, all the time, even though objects would arise, there would be particular qualities and potentialities that could not manifest. That's because there has to be a sense of limits and separateness in order for certain kinds of experience to come into existence.

The Necessity of Limitations

With the inclusion of the Blue node, there arises a sense of limitation and there's a shutting down of all-pervasive feeling. In the Blue node, you feel localized. There's a dampening of the feeling that "I am the doer of everything."

The feeling of being more than the body becomes anesthetized. It becomes the sense of "I am the doer of what is proceeding from this body" and there's no longer the feeling that all knowledge and information that is arising in the field of Consciousness is mine nor that I'm inseparable from all of this. The knowledge that arises in my mind is my own knowledge and then there's what "other" people say and I learn from them.

The experience in the Blue node is that things come from outside or inside. There is then a relative sense of self and a relative sense of others. This is a sense of limits and with it there's a relative subjectivity and a relative objectivity. However, although the Blue node is indeed the sense of the localized human self, there is more to it than that. The potential of the Blue node is to also embody and be filled with the qualities of the Purple and Red nodes. An embodied human life is fulfilled in plumbing the depths of its humanity and its Red and Purple nodes as well, so that they are all lived at once. What I'm calling "Radical Subjectivity" can include relative subjectivity and relative objectivity arising within it. It's still Radically Subjective, but in the Blue node, you also have a relative subjectivity and a relative objectivity inside that Radical Subjectivity.

It is important to understand that relative subjectivity and relative objectivity are a manifestation or unpacking of the potential qualities that were un-manifest in Being but could not be made manifest without the sense of limitation or duality. There are certain potentials, certain qualities, that cannot come into existence unless there is a sense of "other"; that is, unless there is someone else or something else that is separate from them. We cannot really be here, be who we are, or manifest what we are, without a sense of limits. Yet we often wish that there would not be limits.

To love in the truest sense, you have to care for someone else who is not you. In order for Being to experience love in that way, it needs to have limits. To persevere, we need to have a sense that our action is not all-powerful but is our limited action. There has to be a relative subject, an "I," and the power that we have has to be limited. To be brave, to feel bravery, we have to be afraid of losing but to still proceed anyway.

All of these qualities that come forward from Being come forward through limits, and there are countless more qualities that come forward only through limitation. Limits both reveal and conceal. They reveal certain qualities that exist only in potential in Consciousness, that wouldn't come forward without there being limitation. But in the coming forward, they conceal the unlimited nature. Even humanly, our gifts and our burdens are often one and the same thing.

Relative subjectivity and relative objectivity continue to change, they shift around in size and scope. Our sense of who we are keeps shifting. Our sense of what reality is keeps shifting. They're nebulous and the fact is that while their change-ability can drive us crazy it also is the way we grow, the way we expand, and the way we go beyond our relative sense of the current limitation. This becomes important as we look at each of the nodes. There is not a consistent "I" that is the same in each node. Our sense of who or what we are is different depending on what node we're in just as our sense of relative objective reality is different in each node.

Integrity

Limits are also related to our sense of forward motion into a greater sense of integrity. As spiritual human beings, we prefer to be moving forward towards a sense of wholeness. If relative subjectivity is who you are as a relative person—who you take yourself to be, your thoughts, your feelings, your body and everything that you are in the most human sense—then integrity means aligning all of that with what you take to be objectively true or real. However, what you take to be objectively true is of course relative; it's only your current picture of reality. Aligning that with relative objectivity is an ongoing process of constantly balancing and adjusting. Our picture of reality is always changing.

So it's never 100% clear, and that's part of the human experience. We're trying to align our relative sense of ourselves (relative subjectivity) with what seems to be the relative objectivity, but by nature it's never precise. This is appropriate movement toward a horizon that is never reached and it produces a human integrity that is always closer but is never the ideal.

This motion toward integrity is its own reward, but as human beings perfection is never found in time. As mentioned earlier, there are two ways of looking at practice: in one way, you practice in order to arrive at a completely "done" place. That sort of practice that wants to own something is not what this is. Our kind of practice is like that of a musician who practices because practicing is what musicians do; they never expect to be done.

In the Embrace of Limits, Energetic Presence Shines Through

The Blue node is the context in which the unique human life, complete with all its apparent limitations, is continually embraced. When you have a disposition of wanting to embrace everything, you also have an orientation toward being all of it, and an unexpected kind of transformation and even transcendence of limits can happen as a result. But it's not that you are trying to avoid anything, it's that you are simply uncovering the nature of being human. It's not a trick to get beyond it, rather you're uncovering its essence profoundly.

Purple begins to radiate through this Blue because they're not separate. Most of what keeps things stuck is an unconscious (and sometimes a conscious) resistance to being what we experience because it can be uncomfortable or overwhelming. This is entirely understandable and we can't rush this process. It's not about forcing ourselves to be present but rather to gently become aware of how there's a kind of withdrawal from what we're feeling and experiencing. We need to proceed gently and have compassion for ourselves.

During peak experiences, there is sometimes a temporary removal of the blocks that keep us from the experience of genuinely authentic feeling. At such times, Blue ends up touching deeply into Purple. There's a sense of deep authenticity, and in some ways, it's transcendent. It's not transcendent in the Red node sense, but it is going beyond the usual partially shut down feeling that keeps us stuck. So it's not the usual cramped way of being human.

We all fluctuate between feeling uncomfortable and feeling relaxed. Even when our experience is very uncomfortable, if we allow ourselves to feel all that we are and to be present with our humanity, we feel more authentic, and this is a kind of relaxation into all of what we are, into a fuller sense of ourselves.

Sometimes when people experience this kind of deep, genuine feeling, it's as if they don't know who they are anymore. When Purple starts to shine through Blue, it can make us feel incredibly authentic like some new form of the "real me" but we also can seem unfamiliar to ourselves. There can be a sense of, "Who is this? Who said that? Where is my voice coming from?" This combination of letting yourself be with the unknown and applying great compassion for whatever arises is what makes it possible for us to have the Purple shining through the Blue. For me, that's what it means to be truly living the Blue, the Embodied Human. To be an Embodied Human is to reclaim or allow the Red and the Purple nodes to be integrated and to shine through ordinary experience. At the same time, it's not to push away a sense of ourselves that is sometimes very dense. When we're not feeling particularly authentic, we are with that as well. All these kinds of experiences are within the Blue node.

Surfing

From the perspective of the Red and Purple nodes, everything that arises is a kind of magical display of fireworks.

From the standpoint of the Blue node, things emerge as discreet objects. They seem to appear as existing in and of themselves but there is something inherently difficult about that because things are not as they appear.

Everything is always changing, but everything also seems very similar from moment to moment. By analogy to a film, each frame is like a mind moment. According to some meditation masters, each moment comes into existence and then passes out of existence. Each moment arises and is distinct and different from the last, but it's similar enough that we treat it as if it were precisely the same as that which was experienced in the previous moment.

Each moment flashes into existence and then ceases to exist. Then, in the tiniest fraction of time, a new moment comes into existence which is very similar to (but not identical to) the last one and then that moment fades away and then another moment and another moment. There's an ongoing flashing into existence of everything; it's one representation or display of what's possible, of what is potential in Consciousness. With each new frame, all things are continuously changing and shifting, including the sense of our relative subjectivity. Our sense of ourselves at the relative level changes along with everything else that appears as relative objectivity.

With access to the Purple node in the midst of the Blue node, you can contact the way you are a unique display of energy in each moment even as you are the body as well. You can notice that your felt sense of yourself keeps changing. You (in the relative sense) are not simply a separate body/mind. Ideas of ourselves as substantial, continuous, distinct, relative subjects keep us stuck with a concept that shuts out the Purple and Red node experience. At the same time, if we resist such limiting thoughts when they arise, we create conflict within ourselves. It's more helpful to see such ideas simply as ways to interface with the rest of humanity, but not as defining who we are. It's very paradoxical, and life is continuously ironic for a spiritual being who wishes to live the Tapestry of Being.

At the relative level of the Blue node, both our experience of ourselves and of objective reality keep changing, so in an effort to find stability, we may end up treating things as simply things in themselves, as if they were static objects rather than aspects of changing relative relationships. Of course, the limits of this view sooner or later show up, exposing the problems with this pretense, becoming the stuff of surrender.

In terms of health, there are various kinds of medicine, care, and psychology that stem from a limited view of what a human being is, and they treat the body/mind as though it's a static thing to be fixed. In contrast to this approach, when we take into account that everything is always in flux in relationship to systems that are also always in flux, then we are more in tune with the dynamic relative truth.

Within the Red node of the Radical Subject, happiness and satisfaction comes by resting attention in the unmoving space that is the context of everything. Whereas, within relative reality, it's more like surfing, where we're continuously finding a shifting sweet spot rather than hitting a steady target and being finished.

Being What Is

When we embrace what is, and choose what we are and what we already have, it can become a doorway. All feeling, every sensation whether pleasant or unpleasant can be recognized as a form of the energy of the Purple node.

By entering into our feeling as the sensation of the human experience, we become enlivened, we become powerful. This is not done as a trick to go beyond the human limits, but rather an embracing of the human life for what it is at any particular moment.

There is a deep profundity even in sadness if we allow ourselves to enter into it. There is a reservoir of feeling that we can tap into simply by living our lives and feeling what we feel. Even when we don't find ourselves contacting our blissful nature through human activity, we can appreciate what we feel for what it is. This can be extremely nourishing and satisfying beyond the highs and lows of excitement.

A good book, a warm bath, a story, dancing, listening to music, walking in the woods, gardening, watching a sunset, enjoying the feeling of simply breathing. While chasing peak experiences, we can easily overlook life's simplest pleasures. They deserve to be celebrated and appreciated as sacred in themselves, just as they are.

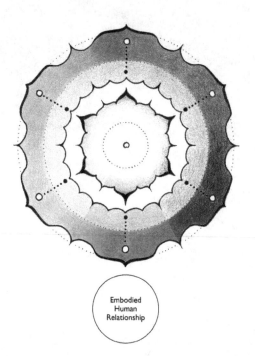

Embodied
Human
Relationship

Chapter 5
The Catalytic Magic of Awakened Relationships

Green: Embodied Human Relationship

So far, we have gone through the three identity nodes of the Tapestry. Those nodes are about the mystery that we all are. The next three nodes are the relationship nodes, in the context of a Spiritual life. In Chapter 1 we said:

Green is the dimension of awakened relating where the multiplicity of the distinct otherness of every human (and every other embodied being) is honored and respected. In relationships, appropriate ways of expression and letting in the truth of others is a continual challenge. Interacting with others in mutual sensitivity as we recognize both our unity and our uniqueness creates a safe container for transformation.

In awakened relationship, unity and uniqueness are both contacted and given their due, and strangely, these are complementary in an unexpected way. There's always simultaneously both unity and uniqueness. Standing in our clarified sense of identity gives relatedness a different quality. In fact, identity becomes even further clarified through relationship.

The simultaneity of unity and uniqueness will be a theme throughout the chapter. The Green piece of awakened relating is about actually honoring both. There's a way in which we are one with others, and there's a way in which we're not. This is a paradox that becomes even more mysterious as we go deeper into the realm of relationship as a form of spiritual work.

Of course, we're relating to other people all the time without thinking much about it, but this is something different. The Blue and Green nodes could be mistaken for being ordinary and mainstream but in this context, the Blue and Green nodes are just as spiritual as the Red and Purple nodes. This is because the way we're speaking about them in the Tapestry is not in the usual way. In the Tapestry, the Blue and Green nodes are the human experience in the context of being Divinely Human. It's a human experience that is, at the very least, in touch with all the other colors, all the other parts of the Tapestry.

So we're approaching our human-ness in a way that uncovers more of who we are than what we usually think of as human capacity. This uncovering goes for human relationships too. Everybody is always naturally relating with each other. We're constantly talking and connecting with other people but in the Green node, it is a particular way of approaching relationship and our human-ness that uncovers profundity. The Green node is relating with awareness, mindful of personal boundaries and our spiritual non-separateness.

Catalyzing relationships as a spiritual process requires an intention to approach them that way and an understanding of identity as described in the previous three nodes, something which is much more encompassing than the ordinary view. It's a way of holding relationship as having the potential to uncover a deeper sense of reality than we're used to, a willingness to be challenged beyond our description of relative reality, of what we ordinarily feel reality to be. In this respect, there are two directions into which you can stretch beyond your comfort zone: from Green into Blue and from Green into Yellow. Relationship can become a door opening into mystery, a door that opens in both directions. In both directions, we are challenged to see things differently.

Green into Blue: Uniqueness

In the ordinary sense of things, we are unique and distinct human beings living in a world of apparently separate objects. At this very human level, we live from and as our relative subjectivity, which is the person we think ourselves to be. We experience ourselves as a person residing in a universe of relative objectivity. That is to say, we live in the world as we think it is, relating to people as we understand them to be. We have reality mapped out in our minds, and that reality appears to us as a world of others and objects, and we relate to it by that internal mental map. Ultimately, the universe and life are far more complex than we can understand, but we negotiate and live life telling ourselves what we think we know as a way to interface with this Mystery.

At this relative level, I know who I am by recounting the stories I've always used to get through this life, such as, "I'm so and so. I was born in a particular time and place. These are my parents. This body belongs to me." That is the level of Blue into Green, and relating in this way—both to life and to other people—is plenty challenging in itself! Since every person is using their own distinct internal map to connect to each other, there are bound to be problems. Even when people have similar minds, there are always differences. So we each live in our own mental world, relating to the actual reality (whatever that is) through the maps, indirectly.

Starting from this point, there is a further possible approach to relationships, in which you go beyond your ideas of people and become oriented to them beyond your mapping of them. This way entails allowing ourselves to remember that we actually don't know who other people are, and never really will, so they remain a mystery. Letting yourself experience others as they are in themselves, rather than the way you think they are or take them to be, calls for continuous engagement.

The Green node is to be in relationship to the mystery of existence itself in a very physical way through human beings. In this Green to Blue stretching, we are not jumping to the transpersonal or transcendent, which would be ignoring the way in which people really do exist distinct from us. We are honoring the way in which this is the world that I live in with other people, not a realm of light or energy. It's just regular people but they are a mystery to me in that I don't have access to their experience so I can't and don't know who they really are. Orienting to people in this way challenges us to reconfigure who we think they are. They are living mysteries that I will meet over and over again as their ever-changing forms. So we are continuously being challenged to get up-to-date with the newest relative reality.

What is revealed here is the way in which each soul is entirely unique and alone. There is the constant reminder that we can only know their reports of their own experience, and as such, they are always other than what we think they are.

That's one side of the Green node.

Green to Yellow: Unity

Then there's an entirely different perspective where you begin to recognize that you are non-separate from other people; that they are aspects of you, or that we are all connected through energy.

Non-separateness is related to another mystery where it goes into the Yellow node, Energetic Presence Relationship. Here, you begin to feel a connection through presence. Green, like each of the nodes, has different shades and is a spectrum bridge between two colors. You cannot distinguish precisely where Green becomes Yellow or where Green becomes Blue. There's a way they blend.

Between the Two

Where Green is close to Blue, it is Teal and where Green is close to Yellow, it is Chartreuse.

Embodied Human Relationship in all its fullness includes being willing to deeply touch your own human vulnerability (Teal) while also being sensitive to the energetic presence of others (Chartreuse). It requires willingness and intention to enter into human relationship in that way, for that purpose; that's what makes it a spiritual exploration and not only a purely human interaction.

By allowing yourself to orient to relating in a way that challenges your notion of who you think you are and who you think the other person is, you are then allowing yourself to live in the sense of not-knowing, of mystery. It's important to honor both the poles—of uniqueness and of unity—on the spectrum and not to sacrifice one for the other. There may be times when we are focusing on one of these poles to the exclusion of the other, but they are both parts of the fullness of relating with awareness.

Honoring Our Boundaries

In our relationships, the Green/Blue aspect is about recognizing distinctions between individuals—the way in which we aren't like others—rather than assuming that everyone else is basically another version of ourselves. We become awake to just how unique each person is. Starting from there, we become able to hear one another and be with one another in our uniqueness. We allow there to be appropriate boundaries between us.

It's important to allow ourselves to feel any mistrust or doubt that we have in the relationship and to share it with the other person or at least acknowledge it to ourselves, and to be honest about our feelings of suspicion and fear. Sometimes in spiritual circles, people may tend to override so-called "negative feelings" about other people, rather than examining them. Some people will feel guilty about their mistrust, or they will do what they can to ignore it and push it aside, rather than honoring it. What we're talking about is not diving into oneness too soon or doing what is sometimes called "spiritual bypassing." We need both roots and wings.

Merging energies or resonating with others in an honest and genuine way needs to be based on a sense of feeling safe. Also, boundaries are necessary for the Green node. If you're going to honor Blue, you're going to honor your human-ness. It's useful to recognize how you've unconsciously merged with others, which we often do out of fear. We want to be part of a tribe. We want to be part of a family and often, when we were young, we had to put aside our feelings of doubt or mistrust in order to be part of the household. Maybe we then got used to the habit of putting aside our fears and discomfort, considering it the price of human connection. Many of us block out these feelings in order to merge with a family, so as to get along with everybody. But if we want to have deeper, authentic, relationships, we must begin to recognize how we've unconsciously and mechanically, merged with other people.

When we are awakening, our desire for truth often shows up as noticing that our habitual ways of relating are not authentic to what we feel. As if we are un-numbing, we begin to notice what doesn't feel right, and that can be quite a shock. Living from our new sense of clarity can be a challenge. At the feeling level, it means that we are willing to be with uncomfortable feelings rather than bypassing them. Affirming your boundaries means being in touch with what you're feeling, honoring your actual experience, even if it doesn't feel great. Eventually, the habit of avoiding what we are feeling starts coming undone, and we see that allowing what we feel to unfold is a natural development that happens in the context of the Space of Awareness. So there is no contradiction or friction between "being a person in relationship" and being the Space of Awareness.

This process proceeds in its own way for each of us when attention is brought to it. For example, when you are with certain people, in the context of honoring your feelings, you may very quickly realize that, "I'm not very comfortable with them. I'm feeling some resentment." Then you bring attention to that feeling, and perhaps it becomes integrated because you notice it isn't actually about them, they just remind you of someone from your past, and they have pushed "a button" or touched an emotional trigger of yours. "Oh I get it, this person talks slowly, and that reminds me of my first-grade teacher." You recognize this emotional connection, and it releases from the past association.

By experiencing in awareness that this particular thing is annoying or creates fear in you, you are honoring and allowing yourself to feel the fear or annoyance or mistrust. And in this way, there is seeing through it, and we start to feel safe. Then it becomes possible and even natural to let those people in but in a way that is different. We allow them to be who they are and we can even actually end up coming into some communion with them.

It all depends on feeling safe and on timing. This process needs intention but it's not effort. Therapy, which is a great thing in itself, allows you to dig into your process to clean things up, and many people find that it works quite well for them. But here I'm talking about a kind of insight that happens naturally, through feeling into what is going on with insight, rather than overriding what you feel.

We have many different kinds of relationships. For example, deep resonance isn't going to happen with everybody but it can occur at the right moment. Sometimes it's surprising when it does happen. You end up resonating into resolution with someone when you didn't think that was going to happen. In contrast to that, sometimes you would really like to have this merging or resonating experience with a particular person but it doesn't necessarily happen. We want to honor the organismic quality of it, how it's a natural thing. It certainly helps to have the intention to resolve and release your contracted feelings around all others, but only in safety. It's subtle.

Opening to Others

We are always free to just place our feeling and attention in the Spacious Awareness in which everything arises. So, in that sense, we can always commune with the Spirit of All and become merged with everything and everyone. We'll look at that when we get to the chapters on the Yellow and especially the Orange nodes. But here in the Green node, we are speaking of something a bit different.

Also, even though we are talking about awakened relating here, it's not only a matter of our one-ness. The way in which bodies and minds are arising in Consciousness Itself is a given foundation of this kind of relating that is the focus of the Purple and especially the Red nodes. In that sense, there is not even a merging or a relationship really, because there is no separation at all. But given this, what does relationship mean in the context of that effortless foundation?

We begin an actual relationship with and through our human-ness, the Blue node of awakened human-ness. In the most human sense, we are individual beings, so it's essential for people to establish and be true to their boundaries, to speak their truth. Real honesty is sometimes counterintuitive for people who want harmony. The irony is that this way of being true to yourself has the potential to create a deeper unity than overriding your feelings does. It requires that you have a sense of yourself at the human level of the energies of body and mind and that you are willing to animate them in the "risky business" of acknowledging and even, at times, expressing how you feel differently than others.

A good analogy for this is a living cell in a body. Each cell in a human organism has a cell membrane, a cell wall. The membrane allows osmosis, fluid going from one cell to the next. There has to be a cell wall that's intact yet not so hard that nothing can pass through. That would be too hard of a boundary, preventing the cell from communing with or receiving nourishment from the cells next to it.

If there's a tear in the wall or membrane, there's no protection. With no wall, there's no individual cell, so it dies because there's nothing to distinguish it from the cells around it. Having boundaries that are porous can be dangerous. Yet, in certain moments, you can be in harmonic resonance with another cell such that you feel as though you're just one cell, like two yolks in one egg. There can then be the feeling of being merged, but it's not forced. It's merely recognized that this is a fellow cell of the same organism and an exchange of energy is taking place.

Feeling safe is the essential foundation of entering into energetic communion with the other and it won't feel like an intrusion if there's a natural communion. The more in tune we are with how we are feeling, the clearer we can be about this. At this point, we are touching on the Yellow node of Energetic Presence Relationship. So those two pieces, both Blue and Yellow, are important to develop for the Green node. The more anchored we are in our Embodied Human Identity, the more we can safely allow the resonance of energetic presence to merge in the context of our human relationships.

However, if you find that you've unconsciously merged with another person at any step, it's important to re-establish your boundary. If you find yourself saying "When I'm with that person I lose myself. I act or feel like I don't know who I am," then it's important to step back, sometimes even spatially, and see where your boundaries are. At this point, some people may use therapy or energy work to clarify their boundaries, and these can be great tools in service to the

Green node.

When you once again feel individuated energetically, you may choose to open up the boundary again and allow yourself to merge and experience the way in which you are one with the other. When it feels right, there really is enough room for everyone to energetically be here together. When you feel safe, you can expand out and be your whole self while still being in the same space with someone else. It's almost a miracle to discover those moments when you can be who you are—fully expressed and allowing yourself to energetically fill the room—while at the same time, someone else can be in the same room and can also fully fill the room. It's quite amazing.

It's as if there were different kinds of scented mists. You could each fill the room with scented mist. One cloud of mist wouldn't come up against the boundary of another cloud of mist and say, "No, I can't go over there." Each would fill the entire room, in the same space. When it feels safe, that's possible. When there's enough room for everyone, then we can all be here in the same space. There's a paradox of being able to merge into the same space and yet have appropriate boundaries and safety. That both/and is really important.

Letting yourself actually hear other people as they are without wanting them to be different helps you to develop a real boundary, a true boundary. If we let others be themselves, we can see what the differences are between ourselves. It's not some sort of a betrayal of harmony or one-ness. A boundary is not a hard thing. It can be soft and gentle, but it's still a real definition. It is a safe place to be in, as an individual.

Part of what is developed in the Green node is the ability to discriminate between how we see someone else as distinct from the person they take themselves to be, while at the same time allowing those differences to exist as you speak together. This is a delicate situation that requires skill to negotiate. The more we can listen to and become aware of who people tell us they are, the more accurately we will see them but it's not always easy.

Respect for Partial, Relative, Personal Truth

All of these paradoxical, both/and boundaries are clarified through natural relating when we also know we are Consciousness Itself, but only if we don't cling to concepts about non-duality. As much as is possible, you allow yourself to listen to the other through the reality that they see. Simultaneously, pay close attention to what you feel as you listen. That is transformational in itself.

For many years I have been connected to Advaita Vedanta communities that revere the teachings of Sri Ramana Maharshi. Those teachings are about The Self or The Consciousness that is aware of all experience. Teachers in that tradition often point to the way in which we are not a person with a story and how seeing beyond (and through) the belief of being an ego with a personal story is so important and a key to freedom. Of course, that is a very Red node teaching.

Some time ago, I was part of a volunteer group that served an Advaita community of awakening people. The teacher noticed that some of the volunteers were not getting along. Even though they "knew" that they "didn't exist," they still had arguments with each other and difficulties. At that time, I was also using teachings on awakened relating and mutuality. The Advaita teacher was a good friend, and he asked me, "Why don't you help them a little bit in this mutuality thing that you do? If you could assist them to relate to each other in a way that is healthy, I'd appreciate it."

I tried to think of how I could describe healthy relating to a group of friends who said that they did not believe there was any real "other" with whom to have a relationship! I ended up saying, "Well, look. Let's sit in a circle and give each person a bit of time to speak. As each person shares, let us each listen with this question in mind: 'What is it like for Consciousness to be this person in front of me?' So, imagine that a man named John Henry shares. As much as possible, listen from the place of 'What's it like for Consciousness to be John Henry?' You're not listening to know whether you agree or whether you disagree with him. You are not interested in whether John's right or whether John's wrong, whether he understands things or doesn't understand things. As much as possible, the only thing that you're listening for is: 'What's it like for Consciousness to be John?' "

Of course, the only one who's an expert on what it's like for Consciousness to be John Henry is John Henry, himself, because he is what Consciousness is when it becomes John Henry. He would be the only one who could say what it's like. That's one way that I convey this, giving the other person the full power to say who they are and for you to hear them as they are saying it from their position. Even when they are not speaking about themselves, they are still telling you what it's like for them to be who they are, they are telling you about their reality. This way of relating works best when we are speaking from our own experience, rather than about theoretical reality.

I always say "as much as possible" because when you're with someone else, you're going to be present to your own feelings and your own sense of things along with the other person's feelings and their sense of things. We are in the space together in which those are happening at the same time. You're discriminating between what you see as real and what they see as real, and you're allowing their reality to be different from yours. You're not trying to harmonize with them, you're letting them be distinct from you and everyone else.

This clarity about differences between you and others is another piece of discriminating awareness. Simply let there be different perspectives to the extent that it's possible. Also (and this is important), to the extent that it's possible, allow yourself to be vulnerable in the face of those different perspectives. As we said earlier, to be vulnerable is not to ignore your sense of safety. You certainly don't have to become vulnerable with someone if you feel they will be abusive. And yet, when possible, allowing vulnerability has a great effect on things.

The context for using Green as a spiritual means, as a way to go deeper, is doing this only with people where you feel safe enough. Then you allow yourself to be vulnerable. What that means is you allow yourself to be with uncomfortable feelings as they arise in the moment. You notice when you're feeling trust and when you aren't. You're honest with yourself about what you're feeling. If you're honest with yourself, when it's time to share—and if it feels safe and appropriate— then you're honest with the other person too, even when it involves telling them about a lack of trust. Saying "I'm not feeling very trustful right now, I don't feel safe" need not be the end, it can be a real beginning.

Being honest about not feeling trusting or feeling unsafe is an honoring of your reality. Without any further effort, you are creating a boundary or having a boundary, in the sense that I was speaking of earlier. It's not so much that you neces- sarily have to set out to create a border. If you are feeling unsafe, intentionally creating an energetic barrier in your mind can sometimes be very good. There are exercises you can do, such as thinking of a circle of light surrounding you or something like that, but this is not necessary for everybody. What is needed, however, is being honest about what you're feeling, even if only with yourself. That's how a boundary naturally comes into being.

It doesn't necessarily mean that what you're feeling refers to anything ultimately real in any absolute sense. It doesn't have to and that's important to remember. This is why I speak about Radical Subjectivity—which is the Ground of Being—as distinct from relative subjectivity and relative objectivity. The relative—both our relative experience of the objective world and our relative subjective sense of our self—is arising in Radical Subjectivity.

We're not making any claims for absolute truth regarding our relative experience of life or ourselves. We're just saying, "This is what appears real to me in my relative subjectivity. This is what seems true to me in my life and so that's the guidance I use in terms of my own life." That's all that's necessary. It doesn't have to be absolute truth. We have to acknowledge our own sense of things, even if it may end up being objectively incorrect. That lets everybody off the hook regarding having to prove anything. All you have to do is be honest about what you feel, without having to justify whether it's reasonable or unreasonable.

There is a safety that is created by the listener if they actually hear you when you are speaking in vulnerability. And in that safety, there is more room to examine your own subjective experience honestly and to look more deeply. There is less at stake when we don't have to defend ourselves. Then we can be more willing to consider our motives and claims with a willingness to see from another point of view. This can happen quite naturally.

For example, you might say, "I feel that you're angry at me and I feel unsafe."

Then the other person might say, "Well, I don't feel angry at you."

Now, if the listener immediately says, "I don't feel angry at you," but you get a sense that they haven't heard you, then it's not going to be enough. If instead, the person waits such that you can feel from your side that they really do understand you're afraid because of your belief that they are angry, you will know they mean it when they say, "I hear you. I get it."

They might even say something like, "I'm sorry you feel unsafe," and you relax and then they may ask, "Can I share something with you when you're ready?"

"Yes, go ahead."

"I want you to know from my side that I actually am not angry at you."

You can let that in and you may be able to hear it. Then there's a kind of reordering of your subjective sense of things so that your earlier thought, "They're angry at me," becomes something else, without any discounting of yourself.

People are often not even aware of what they're feeling. We are not claiming that what we are feeling is the "real" or "ultimate truth." You don't need to do that. We're speaking only in the sense of relative personal truth here. There's a lot of uncovering and richness and deepening that can happen by paying attention to what we feel in the relationship. Just staying with what we feel and listening to what the other person feels can be tremendously transformative.

Each in Their Own Reality

You can understand that every person is living their life from their own perspective. They experience their relative subjectivity and even their relative objective reality differently than you do. There is a way in which each version of reality has validity as being a lived perspective in its own right that is experienced by a living being.

Hearing and seeing the other as they describe their own reality is an important base for awakened relating. Paradoxically, that doesn't mean you hold that another person's view of reality is right for you. While I do feel that each person's perspective is valid in the sense that it is their truth, that does not mean that I think that everyone's truth is equally true. We each have our own feelings about what value another person's perspective has for us. That's our subjective truth. For instance, I don't hold that Adolf Hitler's truth is equal to the Dalai Lama's truth but I will acknowledge that they are both worth listening to.

If we want to understand someone, we have to hear their perspective, no matter how distasteful it is to us personally. We first have to hear how it is for them, from their side. That doesn't mean we have to say, "Oh, that's just as good as anything else," but it can create compassion and connection. It's important when expressing your own feelings, to do it in a way that acknowledges it's your own view but not necessarily the absolute truth. Many people use "I" statements to convey this.

Another important piece of awakened relating is to become aware of your effect upon other people from the way you express yourself. Sometimes we overlook it, or we may think, " I just want to express myself honestly and however it lands is not my problem." But that will break or at least damage the connection in relating. Awakened relating includes letting yourself take in what others say about how they experience what you're sharing, and how it lands in them.

Of course, you also notice the effect upon yourself of what others share, and you can then share that with them. Honest but risky phrases can sometimes help. For example, "When you spoke that way, I felt afraid." Or "When you raised your voice, I felt pushed back." Or "When you spoke softly, I felt pulled forward, and I felt warm towards you." Or "When you were so honest and vulnerable, I felt so much love for you." It goes both ways. Being willing to apologize for the way that you affect others is the lubrication for all of this.

The unusual thing in this way of relating is that you're willing to apologize for the way that you affected others even when it was not your intent to do harm. Sometimes you may need to apologize for actually wanting to hurt someone. For instance, you might be so angry that you are trying to shake them up and get them to feel how serious it is. If they report being hurt by this you might apologize, possibly saying something like, "I'm sorry. I went overboard there. I was trying to affect you, and I shouldn't have gone so far. It was over the top" or "that wasn't respecting you." In that case, the apology is for something that you actually did.

At other times, you might have said something as innocent as, "Hi. How are you?" but in a particular tone such that they felt pushed back by it. In that case, apologizing can be useful even when you didn't intend to do any harm at all. If there were five people in the room and only one of them said that you were being harsh while the others said it was nothing, it would still be good to apologize.

It's important to recognize that intentions are secondary to

effects. For the person affected, the meaning of your communication is the way it landed on them, not the way you intended it. That's sometimes a difficult thing to take in. Sometimes
we end up in a defensive mode and are more interested in our
intentions than in actually communicating with others. At
times, it seems that we're willing to sacrifice the communication, the relationship and the connection in favor of holding
onto our position, "I didn't intend that, and so I'm not going
to apologize for something I didn't do."

We may be aware that the other person is what we consider to be overly sensitive. At these times, we have to remind
ourselves that we are more interested in communicating with
this person than in being right. If we look at every individual
as a species unto themselves, then we can approach each one
in a way that we respect them even with whatever quirks we
feel they have.

Remembering that the goal is actually to connect with
someone helps a lot in doing this form of listening and apologizing. Of course, this means you're going to have to be
willing to notice how your own psychological conditioning,
projections and wounds are present as you're relating. A lot
of psychological material in our Blue node human identity
comes up in relationships. A commitment to approach each
relationship from an awakened but embodied human perspective is a natural way to uncover issues that you may not
have realized were there.

We Each See Every Other Person in a Way That No One Else Does

Now we come to another dimension of relationship that does
not cancel out their "otherness" but paradoxically includes

that "otherness" in further mystery and non-separateness.

In the midst of relationship, we can notice that we each have a unique perspective on others. Only you see someone the way you do. So, there is a way in which everyone you see is non-separate from you. This recognition opens a different dimension or aspect to the relationship, where Green is coming into contact with Yellow and goes beyond the usual way we see each other as individual human beings.

For instance, in your relationship with your spouse or partner, there is a way in which no one else sees or knows the exact same person that you do. No one else knows that one, even your partner doesn't know themself that way. Your partner is experiencing themself from their side, not as you do. You are experiencing them from your side, and nobody experiences anyone else in the same way. So, there is a way in which only you know the person you love.

When you sit with that recognition, it can be unnerving and mysterious. This insight sometimes comes while attending a funeral. You may hear the differences in how people talk about the beloved who has passed. It raises the question, "Who was that person, really?" You realize that they were different to different people. You could not know them as those other people did, but only as the one that you knew. The idea that someone exists as entirely separate from another is flimsy when examined. Who we experience when we "know" someone is in many ways dependent upon us, and is not separable from us. It's very mysterious.

Whoever destroys a soul, it is considered as if he destroyed an entire world. And whoever saves a life, it is considered as if he saved an entire world. — Mishnah Sanhedrin 4:9

There's a way in which every person you see is seen only by you. It's as if you see a version of them that no one else sees. Since you are the only one who can see them in that way, then there is a way in which they are a part of you because nobody else sees them the way you do. In that sense, you are the only one who knows that person, that version of them, and they live only through your eyes.

The unique way in which we see people will go with us when we pass, it will disappear from the earth. You are the only one who is holding that vision of who they are. Because nobody else knows that person in the way you do, they are very, very close to you. To repeat it: when someone dies, you are connected to that someone in a way that's unique to you. And when you die, that particular vision (or version) of the person is lost. This is the preciousness of living beings. When one person dies, a whole world is gone too.

That's one piece of the mystery—how the other is a part of you in your experience of them. But then there is also another piece where you can see the way in which you have no idea what the experience of your partner is from their side. I don't know what it's like to be my partner. I don't have access to her experience so she is a mystery to me. I don't know what her experience is. Only she knows that. Even given every kind of experience we've had together and knowledge that I have "about" her, she remains a sealed mystery to me, in that sense.

There's a way in which we think we know people, but it's not possible to know them as they know themselves. The other in their totality is beyond anyone's ability to know. Truly, people are a divine mystery.

We have a sense of ourselves with which we are familiar. But at times, that sense can shift. There are times we enter into states when we hardly recognize ourselves, such as when contracting in fear, or when relaxing and expanding. Perhaps the most unusual shift is when we expand in our Energetic Presence Identity and notice a stronger, more empowered sense of ourselves. It seems to be almost "other" if we are not used to it. There may be moments in which the voice seems to come from a different place in the chest, and you might wonder who is speaking through you. Yet, it feels like a very authentic natural expression. It's a version of "you" that you didn't know you were, but it feels very right.

There may be times when we're relating to others, that while they are speaking with us, we notice in their voices and their eyes that they're seeing someone who is different from the person we take ourselves to be. In that interaction, they may be drawing forth qualities from you that they see but that you didn't know you had in you. Others can sometimes see us in ways that we don't see ourselves and they can bring that forward in us. What a mystery it is!

Here's an exercise that may assist in understanding what we just covered.

Exercise 1

This visualization might help you get a sense of what may be possible when opening up and sharing from a place of awakened relating. This can be useful to do when you are anticipating a difficult conversation with someone who is a friend.

When you're ready, close your eyes and think of someone you know. See yourself sitting with them and imagine you're having a deep sharing conversation and that you're listening to each other.

At the moment when it's time for you to share your perspective, in that instant when you're about to share your side of the conversation and give your take on how it is, see yourself allowing yourself to forget your side of the conversation and simply feel empathy for them. Just temporarily, for that moment, put aside what you think it all means and gaze empathically. It's as though time has stopped and all things take place in silence.

As you see yourself there, you are feeling safe and opening up your energy and allowing them to be as they are. You can see yourself embracing them energetically, reaching out with your energy, opening up your boundary and taking them into the space in which you both are. Your sense of yourself extends and infuses them and they are also in you energetically as if you are two yolks in the same egg or even one blended yolk. Allow yourself to feel what this is like. Take your time.

Now, see yourself responding in a relaxed way, sharing what you feel. If there is something uncomfortable that you want to share, feel that feeling as you see yourself speaking, and relax into the feeling inside yourself. Accept your own feelings as you see yourself speak. Whatever the other person seems to be feeling as you speak, feel that in yourself as well. Watch as you're sharing together, talking together. As you do this, it's almost as if you're able to feel the other person from inside them.

Feel any comfortable or uncomfortable feelings that you both seem to be having as if they are all part of you too. Those feelings are now yours and you feel them from the inside. Feel them as if they are part of you. These feelings may be different from how you feel, yet they are familiar. You understand them by being them. Allow yourself to register all these in your body now and in your energy. In your imagination, see the two of you relaxing there, hearing each other. Allow the image to dissolve. When you're ready, open your eyes.

Safety and Permission

So much of what we are afraid of is that we will not be accepted; we are concerned that we will be judged.

That is a reasonable fear because in much of our lives, we will be relating to people who may indeed judge us. It's natural that we don't open up to people when we don't feel safe and there is no need to share beyond your sense of safety. However, if you are in a relationship of dedicated mutuality, where you consciously support each other spiritually, then relating becomes a bit more delicate because you are committed to entering in the midst of vulnerability.

In the context of a circle of support, we might internally judge ourselves before others judge us. We then shut down or censor ourselves as a preemptive defense. We would prefer to reject ourselves or the feelings that may come up rather than even try the possibility of being accepted by somebody else. We think, "What if they judge me? That may hurt, so I'll judge myself first." An approach I sometimes take, when it feels safe enough to do it, is to come forward and speak from my vulnerability. I'll just state upfront what my fear is about the interaction, and that can diffuse things right away—but even to do that requires a certain degree of safety.

I often tell people that to find the real edge of safety, we have to go a little bit past it. Whenever the feeling of not being safe arises, I suggest you pull back into a space of feeling safe. I know some people will say, "Well, no, that's the place to push ahead, that's your edge, so go past that edge." I don't suggest that. I suggest that you step back so that you feel safe again and have time to catch your breath. Then, when safety has been re-established, you can dare a bit again, if you want. If it feels right, you can regularly re-check to see if you can risk further and take the communication further. This way of daring goes with much in the awakened life, including relationship and communication.

Sometimes we're afraid and need to take our time before

we regroup and try again. Honoring your sense of what feels safe to you is paramount, and then what's next can follow. Sometimes it's evident that, at least for now, that's as far as we should go. Sometimes, we just don't have permission to go any deeper, and that's ok too.

Be with This Person Now

Exercise 2

This exploration will help you to see how we unconsciously carry over and project past images when we relate. We'll do this by consciously exaggerating our tendency and recognizing our power to discriminate and choose.

When you're ready, close your eyes. Imagine a problem or a difficulty you had recently in a relationship with someone that you know. It should be a time recently when you felt that you were not seen as you are or were not heard, or maybe even were hurt in the exchange. Remember what happened there, feeling into how that feels for you to be hurt and not seen. Include any additional feelings of disappointment you may still have when you think about this event, such as resentment, any sense of hindrance, insult, maybe outrage. Increase the feeling a bit, intensify it a bit, exaggerate the feeling a little.

As you're feeling disappointment and resentment and hindrance, insult, outrage, how does the other person look to you when you're feeling those things? What other images come up about this person when you're feeling this? What other adjectives arise in you for what this person is doing or how they're being? Just allow them to arise and be there.

Now, as you remember this image and the feelings that you're having around this person, notice if it's at all familiar. Does this feel like something that happened before in your past?

See if you notice how it's like a feeling that you've had with someone else from your past, or similar events that have happened in your life. What is it like from your younger self? Feel the connection from the past. Take your time.

Now, allow yourself to see that feeling as being removed and separated from the person that you're relating to now. Be with this person now.

When you're ready, open your eyes.

Keeping Relationships Current

What benefits to yourself can you find by allowing yourself to see without the negative imagery from your past? This reminds me of the phrase, "People change, and then they forget to tell each other." Instead, see them as they are now. The key here is to be aware and to use discrimination. Our unconscious projection of negative feelings onto other people keeps us from connecting with them. We're not making it a rule that you must always drop your negative feelings but it can help your process if you give yourself a chance to see when those negative feelings are connected to somebody who isn't present now.

Of course, there's always a risk. It's daring to lower your guard and find out if this person is indeed who you take them to be. However, in another sense, there's also a risk in not lowering your guard and maybe missing out on the opportunity to connect with somebody because you have a sense that they're not safe. In both cases, you're daring to trust yourself. Either you trust yourself not to trust them, or you trust yourself to give it a try and provisionally trust them. No one else can ever relieve us of this responsibility. The key is to be conscious and to recognize that we sometimes create feelings or associate feelings with people that have nothing to do with them right now. However, sometimes we might find ourselves thinking; "This behavior has been a pretty consistent pattern, and I'm not interested in lowering my guard because it seems appropriate and safer for me not to." That's the whole organic piece and the naturalness that this is.

This is not a formula. The mind is part of the experience but it need not define the experience. In this sense, there is also a deep appreciation for the mind and mental images and the place they have in relationships. Like spices in a dish of food, they can bring out the richness and add flavor but also like spices, the mind should not overwhelm and define that of which it is a part. There are many times when our experiences from the past add richness to our interactions with people now. Again, this is about becoming conscious. Imagery and feelings connected to what happened in the past can be a very profound part of the present.

This isn't something you can figure out beforehand; it's something of which to be mindful and curious. It could very well be that you usually see people exactly as they are, new every moment, but with something as subtle as mind projections, we're conscious of them only when we are. This is practical rather than theoretical knowledge. It's not like turning a switch on or off, doing it or not doing it. Rather, it's insight to be developed over time. We don't expect to get this insight perfected and knowing for certain that we are always seeing people as they are but we are becoming more and more conscious of this, more and more aware of the way that the mind produces images.

We just notice, and that's enough. The thing about the Green and Blue nodes is that development is intentional but gradual, not spontaneous or instantaneous, and there is no final end to it. We maintain an endless but relaxed vigilance.

This way of staying current makes for good relationships but also, with a different emphasis, it can occasionally happen in such a way that it even leads to transcendence of all concepts.

Paradoxical Transcendence through Relationship

The Green node starts from a very embodied, human and earthy place, proceeding from the Blue node. It's recognizing the other person as another living animal, another mammal with all that entails. Once there's been a negotiation of boundaries, and a certain level of safety has been met between you, then there's a natural inclination to open up energetically and to feel at the level of presence. The Green node continues from the Blue, human dimension to expand and include the energetic presence dimension of relationship, which is the Yellow node.

Here, there are at least two ways the transcendence of conceptual mind can take place in the context of relationship. In the first, in the very human reality of being with people as they are, we can remember how unique and alone each one is, and ultimately see the fact of their unknowable-ness for us in terms of their own experience. We cannot know what it is like to be them.

Then there is the way in which we can contact each other at the level of our presence or energy. That is also a transcendence of the known into a moving beyond our separate sense of identity as we merge energetically. It requires being willing to be with the unknown in the face of this energy field that we are relaxing into together. You begin to move into a form of meditation while relating with each other. Moving into silence, into a sense of presence in which you are not separate, a natural quieting of the mind while listening.

When you're present with someone, if you can recognize whatever images and feelings are arising as you listen and just let them go and flow through, you are allowing yourself to be in the now. In that moment you are not referencing your present experience with them through thoughts of the past.

It doesn't matter whether those images and feelings are accurate or not. What matters is that when the actual person is right there, their presence now is who they are, so we can let go of thoughts, even good ones. The slate is clean any time we ignore thinking and just feel what is in this instant, in silent listening—letting yourself simply be in the space in which the relating happens. From here, you can also let go of the person you think you are as well; there's no need for thought in this space of silence, of feeling together.

At any moment you can allow yourself to take a deep breath and let go of who you take anyone to be and allow them to be who they are. To the degree that it's possible, forget about what you think you know because it's not necessary to bring it here. Immediately, you may feel more of a connection to them and a willingness to not know who they are or who I am. Thoughts about what's right, what's wrong, or who's right, who's wrong, fall away for now.

I want to be clear that this is appropriate only if and when we have already become comfortable regarding our boundaries. It is from that basis that we can move in and out of the conceptual mind, in touch with the way we are simultaneously both distinct and non-separate, neither avoiding nor clinging to either way of being.

The Blue/Green way of relating is endeavoring to be real with others so that you feel that you are in good communication with other people. You have some sense that you are being seen and heard by others and some sense that you've

seen and heard them. You have the feeling that you understand each other. When this is happening with people you
trust, then you feel that you can check your sense of relative
objective reality with them, and you can know that you are at
home in life.

When we are up-to-date with friends, we feel reassured
that we, in our subjective personality, are in alignment with a
shared sense of objective reality. As a relative human, we need
that reassurance, and it gives us balance. Getting clear here is
not merely consoling ourselves with the knowledge that we
have friends who love us, though that in itself is valuable. In
order to have the solid footing we want, we must be in touch
with people as they are now in present time, rather than the
image we have of them in our heads.

We need to be able to be free in relation to the
image-making mind—both free of it, and free to use it. We
need the image-making or imaginal mind; it is necessary for
human beings. The imaginal mind is an expression of being;
it's not a mistake. So, we're not trying to live without the imaginal mind. Having an image of people is a necessary part of
negotiating through life. It's a useful development and it's a
placeholder when the person is not there. We think of the image of them, and we have feelings about it as a proxy, but it's
not who they are in their totality right now.

The point is to exercise the mind consciously and use it ju-
diciously. It's quite mysterious though. The image, itself, has
a lot of power; although people are not the image we have of
them, there is some energetic power in our pictures of them.
Our internal image of individuals sometimes affects them
and conversely, sometimes people can affect us through the
image we hold of them. It's mysterious beyond explanation
and goes to the root of our Energetic Presence Relationships

and our interdependence.

There's a way in which others are part of our self, and there's a way in which they're not. For me, it always starts with letting others be what they are rather than what I imagine they are. But that's just where it starts.

Indra's Net

There's a great image from East Indian mythology, known as the Jeweled Net of Indra. Indra is a chief god in ancient Indian scripture. Imagine a huge net; at every place where the cords of the net intersect, there's a multifaceted jewel that has perfect mirror-like surfaces. Each jewel in the net perfectly reflects every other jewel surrounding it. We are each a Jewel.

So, the reality for all of us as sentient beings is a huge cosmic net stretching into infinity. Every jewel reflects all the other jewels around it so that all of them see themselves in the jewels around them. This is how it is for us, we see ourselves through each other. We have a sense of ourselves. But we can gain a deeper sense of ourselves by connecting with other people who give us a different sense of ourselves. There's a way in which we are interconnected and even a way in which we are one. At the same time, we have no access to the experience of any other jewel except as they are reflected in us.

You see and know only the "me" that you can see but you don't see any other "me." In that way, we are a sealed mystery to each other. In that sense, you are never actually seen and heard by another, at least not in your totality. But we can sometimes feel that we are truly known by someone. So what, exactly, is happening at those times? Being seen and heard is a feeling sense of energetic resonance in which we're being allowed to be who we are and are being appreciated by someone, which brings the subjective feeling of being understood. Sometimes it takes a lot of words and evidence that we are being understood in the conversation—a lot of back and forth—while at other times it takes only one word, or even no words.

Being understood or being seen and heard, is a feeling of resonance, but it's rarely spoken about that way. What's usually assumed is more like, "Somebody heard me and understood me. Finally, they know what I'm like." But when you think about it, nobody can see and hear you from your inside. They don't know what it is like to be you. But when they speak in such a way that you recognize you're being allowed to be who you are, there's a feeling of resonance. They are allowing whatever is happening right now, there's total validation for it, and there's no manipulation going on, no interference going on. There's just letting you be how you are, and there's a feeling sense of resonance. No matter what is said, no matter what the words are, it can even happen in silence. You can feel it sometimes, and no one even needs to say a word, but you feel seen and heard. That feeling of resonance is the sense of love, and it is a tuning into relating through energetic presence.

Here is where the Green node begins to move into the Yellow node and this is really about energy. It's not only about the person who's listening to you and what exactly they physically say or do. It's more about the way they're listening to you that helps you relax into a particular kind of energy field together, so you are in a certain kind of resonance. You are then resting in a special kind of presence of well-being that's inherent in you already but the person helped you to directly relax into it through their acceptance of what is.

Love and Gratitude

It's good for our process to be supremely grateful to all the others in our life who stimulate and activate love in us. Energetic presence is within us, so it's not something that simply arises from outside sources. Still, that which is within us is drawn forward, stimulated and amplified from outside by those who love us, so it's natural to be thankful to everyone who does that for us. The recognition that they're touching, triggering and stimulating something that's already inside us, is an important key. It's something to really let in.

Here's a guided exploration about how being seen and heard or loved allows an energetic presence to be activated or stimulated within you.

EXERCISE 3

When you are ready, close your eyes. Think about a time when you felt deeply loved or cared for, really seen and understood or deeply appreciated by someone. Allow yourself to remember exactly what that was like and let in the feelings that you felt in the midst of this love. See through your own eyes. See what you saw, hear what you heard, feel what you felt. Take your time. Allow yourself to continue to experience this loving moment as you notice the feelings in your whole body, all throughout your bodily energy when you feel loved. Notice whatever full and warm feelings there are.

Take your time and enjoy this.

When you are ready, think of other times in your past when you felt similar feelings or exactly the same feelings with a different person and merge the feelings. These feelings coalesce together. Stay in touch with the feeling and notice that this is a feeling that is yours. Amplify it. Notice what you're feeling in your chest.

Allow yourself to find another similar event in your past that may have been even more subtle or more pleasant in which you felt loved. Allow yourself to bask in it.

Can you imagine stimulating your own energetic presence like this with feeling and going through your life with it as often as you like?

What effects do you feel it would have on the rest of your life and the people that you meet and people that you see?

When you're ready, open your eyes.

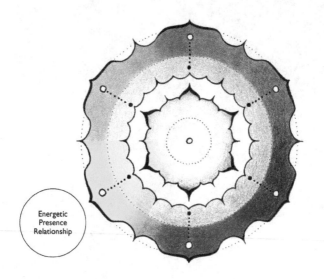

Energetic
Presence
Relationship

Chapter 6
Unseen Help: Becoming Sensitive to Numinous Presences

Yellow: Energetic Presence Relationship

There are many ways to contact the Spirit of Guidance. When I teach or hold a sitting, I often like to start off with a Tibetan chant called the 7-line song. I learned it long ago, and it has been very important in my life. It is an invocation to Padmasambhava, who is said to have been the first Tantric Guru or Lama to come to Tibet. This chant invites this legendary figure—also known as Guru Rinpoche—to be present. Guru Rinpoche came from the northwest of India, probably from what is now the Pakistani Swat valley, in the 8th century. At this point facts about his life have been blended with myth and symbol to such a degree as to be inseparable.

Although the chant is addressed to the historical man Padmasambhava, I was taught that Guru Rinpoche also represents the totality of all the teachers who have taught you the indestructible ("Vajra") Truth, particularly your main (or "root") teachers. Padmasambhava is the accumulated composite of all of those teachers and stands for, or is a symbol of, that Principle which guides us through everything.

So, when I chant this song, it is an invocation of the very

principle of guidance. Invoking Padmasambhava is a means to invoke your own internal teacher and guidance, as well as whatever external teacher or teachers you may have now.

I mention this because, in the context of a non-dual perspective, invocation or prayer contains a larger and more complex picture than merely calling on "outside" help. The paradoxical way that inside and outside are not entirely separate makes every invocation and relationship a calling on something that is already an inner resource.

A MEDITATION

Sit in a way that's comfortable for you. Your body preferably upright and relaxed in a way that feels good for you.

Your spine should be more or less straight. Your eyes closed, or if you prefer, they can be open in a very soft way. Easy. Just notice whatever you're feeling right now. To whatever degree you're feeling a kind of presence, or transmission, or radiance, relax with that.

Even if it's simply the energetic presence of your own body that you feel, then relax with that. Whatever sense of energetic field, whatever sense of transmission that you may be feeling, just be with that.

Now your ears: be open and listening to that field of radiance, presence, and transmission. Place your hands in a position that feels open and relaxing into the field of radiance, presence, and transmission. Feel into, and open up, and relax your whole body into the field of radiance, presence, and transmission.

Relax your heart, lungs and entire chest, deeper into the field of presence and transmission. Relax your lower organs, your ribs and solar plexus and navel and belly, sex organs, your hips, eyes, knees, your legs, your ankles and feet and toes, deeper and deeper into the field of presence and transmission.

Relax your entire spine, your back, your shoulders, and all the upper body parts: your chest, upper arm, elbows, forearm, wrists, hands, fingers, neck, throat, your whole face including your nose and your eyes and your eyebrows and your cheeks, your jaw and entire head.

Relax everything deeper into the field of Transmission and presence. Relax every part of you into the current of feeling—whatever energy you're feeling—relax your whole body simultaneously.

You don't have to do anything at all with any of your body parts or with your mind; just relax, just let your breathing and your mind and everything else simply be what they are. Every part of the body is relaxing into the feeling of indefinable energy, presence.

Allow this feeling and transmission to shade and shift and change and affect your body, your mind, and your own energy as it will. Even the intention to feel, you can release into the feeling of transmission, as well as the feeling of presence. Let it all just be what it is.

When you're ready, if your eyes are not already open, you can open them now.

A Story

As I remember it, it's a story inside a story.

One day, Buddha was with an assembly of disciples and was telling the story of another monk and how he also became a Buddha in the distant past. A king named Dharmakara renounced his throne and resolved that he, himself, would become a Buddha in a future life. Dharmakara vowed that, when he became a Buddha, he would manifest an entirely pure dimension that would be the perfect place to be trained in the Dharma and invite any and all beings who remembered him to be reborn in his pure land.

Dharmakara, through countless lifetimes, accumulated so much power through his good karma and wisdom, that when he fully awakened and became the Buddha known as Amitabha, he also then naturally manifested an entire pure realm dimension around him. The nature of this pure land is to be an environment that continuously teaches and transmits the Dharma twenty-four hours a day. Amitabha, according to this story, is no longer just his manifested body, but is in some sense inseparable from the entire pure dimension, or Buddha-land, that he manifests.

This land is a realm of light, and the name, "Amitabha," means "infinite light." So, the whole dimension is like translucent stained glass—it's a multicolored, ever wondrous Buddha-field where everything is always transmitting to you, translucently.

There are many beautiful details described about this pure land. For instance, there are always various kinds of magnificent birds of different colors—swans, peacocks, parrots and the legendary Kalinka bird. Six times every day and night all those birds sing in melodious tune, and the people there hear the Dharma taught within the songs of the birds. They listen to the teachings on the Five Virtues, the Five Powers, the Seven Bodhi-paths, the Eight Noble Truths, and other Dharmas of that kind. After having heard that singing, the living beings in that land quite naturally find that they invoke the Buddha, the Dharma, and the Sangha as a result.

It is through those birds that Amitaba Buddha miraculously manifests with the desire to spread the voice of the Dharma. When, in that Buddha-land a gentle breeze happens to blow, the precious trees in rows and the gemmed nets emit a fine enrapturing tune, and it is just as if a hundred thousand musical instruments were playing at the same time. Everybody who hears that music naturally conceives the thought to invoke the Buddha, to invoke the Dharma, and to invoke the Sangha. It is said that this Buddha-land is arrayed with such good qualities and adornments that by its very nature, it draws everyone to Truth.

Buddha then went on to explain that countless Buddhas are continuously manifesting Buddha-fields that interpenetrate each other. At another time, Buddha taught that all the Buddha realms exist for the sole purpose of leading those born into them to their own Buddhahood. What appears to them when they are there is directly related to them, personally; what they see while there is no accident at all and what they learn there is tailor-made specifically for them, every detail being manifested just for them.

The nature of the pure realm is, according to this story, that when you are there, everything you see around you is alive and teaching and transmitting to you. For those who are in the Pure Land, if they can penetrate their situation and recognize that their own body is a visible part of this dimension, then they find that they are inseparable from all of it. Such a perfect realm seems almost too good to be true. A place perfectly designed to teach us and transmit the Dharma exactly as we need it? Wow, that would be ideal, wouldn't it?

Buddha makes it clear to his disciple, Sariputra, that the Pure Land is possible because of the purity of the Buddha's intention to manifest a place that would precisely serve those beings who have turned to him. So, when Sariputra heard the story of Amitabha's pure land, he was fascinated by Amitabha's awe-inspiring majesty, and the thought came to him, "If a Buddha land is pure because of a pure mind, is it because the mind of this Buddha is not pure that this world is so unclean as we see it now?" In other words: "Well, what about you, Master? Why did you manifest this kind of a realm? It would be so much nicer to be in one of those amazing pure ones."

Interesting question. For me, on hearing this story, my own question is, "What would it be like to live in a universe which is always communicating and transmitting spiritual truth, and where everything is alive?"

Sensitive to Numinous Presences

This is the node where we uncover and develop our capacity to know that we are never alone. Here, we reclaim our heritage as residents of a spiritual universe, becoming sensitive to the numinous, and able to contact unseen help.

This Yellow dimension is the node of our awareness of, and our relationship with, the presences of both incarnate and discarnate beings: angels, saints, masters, guides, buddhas, bodhisattvas, gods, goddesses, nature spirits and departed loved ones, as well as the spiritual or energetic presences of people who are alive now but who are not in our physical proximity.

As we begin to notice the way that all these beings are aspects of One Being or One Presence, we are then moving in the Amber zones and approaching the Orange node of devotion.

Mirror Nodes

A noteworthy feature of the Mandala is that the identity nodes (Red, Purple and Blue) and the relationship nodes (Green, Yellow and Orange) mirror each other. The three first nodes (the identity nodes) are affected by and also affect their mirror relationship nodes, and vice versa. In this case, the Yellow node (Energetic Presence Relationship) is related to the Purple node (Energetic Presence Identity). The more developed you are in your own energetic presence Identity, the more you have the capacity and potential to become sensitive to Energetic Presence Relationships. You can become tuned into other people's energy and the energies of discarnate beings, and the more you work with those links, the more you develop or uncover your own energy field.

Boundaries

There are three aspects of the Yellow node. First, there is a spectrum of experience that's related to the energetic presence of persons, places, and things. Next, there is a range of experience that involves directly communicating with a discarnate or spiritual presence. And finally, there is the experience of realizing that all the various energetic presences that exist are aspects of One Energy.

We'll go further into this subject later, but for now, while we are dealing with the first two aspects of the Yellow node, I think it's important to emphasize that we must stay aware of our boundaries, even as we open to each other.

In all relationships, it is most important for there to be respect, dignity and clear boundaries. The bliss of an energetic connection can be intoxicating, so it's essential that we continue to be mindful and responsible for our process and our lives.

Much of what we spoke about in the previous chapter on embodied human relationship also applies to this node as well, even with the addition of an energetic component here. So, for example, you don't merge too quickly—rather, you respect boundaries and you check your internal sense of appropriateness. By doing this, you are actually allowing the other being to be who they are, and you are also allowing yourself to be who you are. Then, whatever kind of connection happens, it is based upon that authentic foundation, and there may indeed be a big opening in which you feel a merging with someone energetically. But that happens from a place of safety, and it happens naturally, it's not something you have to create.

You may have a profound energetic presence relationship with a teacher and you may be very grateful for it. The development of that connection, when you are actually with them—learning to open to it, learning to breathe into it, and be with it—can be significant. Then, there may be the further development of tapping into their transmission even when they are not present physically, by using a picture or photo of them, visualizing them, or just bringing them to mind. In all of this, such a powerful connection should never lead you to give away your own power without realizing it. A powerful transmission, like any powerful attraction, should enhance your field and not be used by anyone as a means of controlling you.

This degree of caution is very necessary whether you are working with a teacher like a guru, or with a discarnate being. In either case, trust should be earned, based on more than just the powerful energetic connection.

Sometimes, that connection can become stimulating in the kind of way that we usually experience only in an intimate relationship. Your energy is opened and even if you never consummate the relationship physically, there can be a sexual feeling to it. In themselves there is nothing wrong with any of these relationships in energy or presence—in fact, they are often important signposts for us, but we should be conscious of the dynamics of energy and power. These experiences are primarily for your opening and are meant to add empowered energy or grace to your field.

This is a sensitive subject because such openings are an important part of many people's awakened life. There can be a very big opening to a particular person or even to many people, and you might feel as though you've fallen in love. This can pull forth energies from you, and change your life.

However, in all those relationships, the Green node aspect is still very much there, with its inherent issues regarding boundaries and merging and the need to feel safe. Reminding yourself to be clear about your boundaries and being willing to say "no" is essential for your integrity. Even being willing to miss out on an experience because you didn't feel safe is an important sign of spiritual maturity. Opening, in these special relationships, and allowing in and merging, absolutely require the same kind of integrity that is needed in any other embodied human relationships.

Responsible Affiliation with Teachers

When it comes to spiritual teachers, it's crucial that you feel safe. In the Yellow node, it's not required to open up to every individual you meet. If you are really in touch with the way in which the larger field connects us, then, by all means, merge with that wider context and in that way, merge with everyone. That level moves into Orange, but the distinction is worth noting: you are merging with the wider context, not only with the Teacher or with a particular person.

There are many different possible cosmological maps of the Yellow node that may be helpful. Yellow is not about any one particular belief or any special spiritual system, yet it's the realm in which any of those views and systems are possible. It's not about choosing one particular description that is true for everyone; it's more about finding what naturally happens for you, personally.

Yellow is also not ever about forcing yourself to open up to a spiritual presence, either—that would be just as harmful as it would be to force yourself to open to other human beings. I think we need to remember this all the time but it's somehow easier to remember these things when the relationship is an ordinary human relationship and when you consider the other person to be a peer. You must be especially careful if you feel, "This is a person unlike any other, and I'll be missing out if I don't open to them."

When it's a Tantric awakening of our sexual and heart energy, or when there's a spiritual teacher involved, then we can sometimes forget that we need to take care of our sense of safety. Being cognizant of what we're feeling all the time is more important than any ideas we may have about opening.

Other "Entities"

Again, the Yellow node is not about particular beliefs or spiritual systems, although it can include them. For example, some people feel very comfortable with Native American spirituality—connecting with nature spirits or connecting with animal spirits—while other people don't. Some people are drawn to teachings that include invoking ancient gods and deities from Egypt, Syria or Greece and they may want to keep those practices alive. This may also be true for people who describe themselves as Wiccan. Still others are attracted to Ascended Masters.

Some people will be attracted to Tibetan and Hindu spirituality, buddhas and bodhisattvas, gods and goddesses. And of course, there are those who are in touch with the Saints and Angels or Jesus and God the Father. These people may be quite naturally drawn and attracted to all of those beings, and feel very safe opening to those energies. That's what they are attracted to, so that's what they do. These are all examples of what we're talking about in the Yellow node, and there are many other examples as well. Some people are not going to be attracted to any of these, but for those who are, that's beautiful.

In all of this, it's always important that you pay attention to what it is that you, personally, feel and what it is that you, personally, are attracted to regarding energy and transmission. The Yellow node is not, in itself, about any particular system. Everyone relates to it differently.

Connected to the All

The essence of the Yellow node is the spontaneous and cultivated feeling of connectedness, energetic reception, merging, and transmission, which is sometimes called "Spirit communion." It's basically an amplification of our transmission and radiance through feeling, in a relationship with what appears to be another being.

This can take very different forms for different people, yet what is common to them all is that whatever form is used, it's a template to orient us to the mystery. The form it takes is profoundly personal but, if you are moved to work with traditional imagery, I'd advise learning about what the traditional deities are, at least as a starting point. The Yellow node is not about having to believe any of the myths or mythic thinking literally, but it doesn't exclude that either. Also, one can enter into this realm without using any kind of ancient or traditional imagery at all.

Is This Just a Distraction?

In many traditions such as Theravada Buddhism and Zen, there can be a dismissal of visionary experience. These paths are more exclusively Red node, Transcendental Divine Identity traditions. In their effort to focus on that one specific node, they usually dismiss Yellow node or Energetic Presence Relationship events or, at least, they tell you not to pay too much attention to such things because visionary experiences can be a distraction from that Red node focus.

At the same time, in the Theravada scriptures—which are the Pali Suttas of the Buddha—there are many examples of visionary experiences and Yellow node events. For example, the Buddha was said to have had teaching conversations with his deceased mother and communication with gods and goddesses. So, it's there in the Pali Suttas, and even more so in the later Mahayana sutras.

You usually can't convince people who are in a particular tradition or school that's focused in a special way, that it should be okay for them or their school to become open to visionary experiences. It's really up to each person, individually. From my perspective, we—as mature practitioners in the 21st century—don't have to convince anyone about what we do or give a sophisticated reasoning about why.

An experience just pulls you. For instance, you may have heard a voice, and this is meaningful to you. If you know how to work with visionary experience, then you can make use of such things. Various shamanic practices use trance states—whether induced by psychoactive medicine plants or without them. Hypnotic music, dance, ritual, or chanting, are all ways of touching into these states. Sometimes, when we've accessed a non-ordinary state, we can contact dimensions that appear to have countless beings from other realms, and that can feel somewhat like walking into a crowded room.

The challenge is to integrate the experience so that it serves you. That way, we are not merely fascinated by it, but it contributes to our development. Often, simply becoming aware of the fact that there really are spiritual presences can be so mind-blowing that people can't integrate it. Then that becomes an issue in itself. So I can understand why some paths try to avoid the Yellow node, even if they don't explicitly deny that it exists. However, there are traditions that have worked with—and continue to work with—this dimension skillfully and if you do know how to work with it, it can be extremely useful and productive overall.

Does the Relationship Go Both Ways?

Many of us have had a relationship of devotion or prayer that has given us comfort even without the sense of a tacit spiritual communion. But the experience of Shakti, grace or transmission, is what makes an Energetic Presence Relationship powerful. A common situation is having at least some sense of presence when we pray or think of a deity, saint, guru or spiritual being, but without having any clear sense of being "answered," or even a sense that they (whoever they may be) are aware of us.

It's the back-and-forth, reciprocal quality of Energetic Relationship that makes it both so scary and so transformative. One way to initiate this kind of relationship is by responding to a presence or energy that you already feel and then enhancing that feeling by giving it attention. There are all kinds of ways to give the relationship care, and one way is just to think about it—that is, you can use your imaginal mind. I prefer the term "imaginal mind" rather than "imagination" because modern Western culture associates "imagination" with fantasy and entertainment.

We can intentionally cultivate this imaginal aspect of mind. At first, it will seem that something is happening only from your side. There can be an undercurrent of the thought "I feel the need to pray but is my prayer being answered? I'm not sure that I'm feeling anything coming back." When I was growing up, I was not taught to connect prayer with energetic presence but later in my life that kind of connection was "the difference that makes the difference." Now, I very much feel that I am actually in a relationship with the energetic presence of these beings. An Energetic Presence Relationship means that it's not only that I am communicating to them, but that they are also communicating back to me. It may sometimes be simply a communication of love or grace, rather than a revelation of information or guidance, but I'm receiving it.

We have to examine the unspoken taboo in this. Historically, in Western monotheistic traditions, people who let it be known that beings or things talked back to them were sometimes turned in to the authorities by their neighbors or even burned at the stake. The message was that you are allowed to show devotion outwardly, but make sure that you get no response.

You can pray in front of a statue in church as much as you want, but if the statue somehow starts to answer you directly, then you're in trouble. (One of the main differences between western monotheistic traditions and many of the Eastern traditions is the degree of mystical experience you are allowed).

In the West, you could receive an answer, but you'd have to be quiet about it. People couldn't be overly vocal about it, but sometimes it was politically okay if approved by the authorities. We do live with that legacy so, at a deep level, it doesn't feel safe to allow ourselves to receive the message back until we are convinced that it's really okay.

Although I may be contacting something, and although that interaction can really be happening, we don't have many traditions of training in the West that take this seriously. The West did have traditions like this thousands of years ago, but they became widely suspect after the establishment of Christianity. The Church considered receiving direct revelation subversive. This left official Christian authorities to interpret past religious teachings, texts and doctrines without any competition from those who might claim spiritual or otherworldly help.

Hollywood films have saturated us with the implication that you could be a witch if you start getting answers or revelations. In many of those movies, invoking spirit is evil by definition, as in "People played with the Ouija board, and you know what happened." We shouldn't underestimate the unconscious effect this may have on us. That type of social conditioning creates a part of us that may put limits on our openness to relationship with spirit. We may have policed ourselves, so the only guidance we received is from the outside authorities and we didn't trust the Yellow node unless it was the official brand of our church or religion, or approved by it. Perhaps uncensored communication was allowed to go in only one direction during prayer, and that direction was from you to God or the saints. The idea that you would be able to receive direct personal communication from God or the saints may have been looked at with distrust or disdain. So, that door may sometimes be partly closed on our side, through fear. We may have put up walls because we need to trust and feel safe in order to open, and that shouldn't be rushed. Gentleness and patience with ourselves as we take our time to stretch our senses is needed here.

I write this knowing that we live in a world filled with new age spirituality, channeled teachings and spiritualists. My words here are for the awakening people coming from a non-dual perspective who would like to make sense of and develop their own encounters with otherworldly sources. In my experience, this takes both openness and honesty. What I'm pointing to is a profoundly personal process, and we should be careful and skeptical of those who come to us making claims of any sort. Other people's words may inspire us, but cultivating our own capacity for Energetic Presence Relationship is essential in the Yellow node.

The Transcendent Creates Safety in the Midst of the Relative

For me, a fuller sense of the Yellow node didn't develop until the Red node was very firmly established. The basis of non-duality is to be awake to the Subjectivity of Consciousness Itself, the Ultimate Subjectivity. That Ultimate Subject is the same for all of us; it is free of content and is the ground of our being as relative subjects. This is the foundational understanding of the Red node.

The other two nodes of identity (Purple and Blue) are forms of relative subjectivity. They change, and they are objects of Consciousness Itself. Consciousness is aware of our relative sense of ourselves, whether that be our sense of ourselves as an expanding and contracting energy field, or as a human body/mind. Whether we experience ourselves as matter or as energy, both of those options are not stable or invulnerable in the way that Consciousness is.

The importance of what I call "Radical Subjectivity" is in being fundamentally established in the Ground of Being—the Subject of Subjects—rather than in just a relative subjectivity. But we can also simultaneously identify with our Energetic and bodily identities as they arise. Even when we are feeling the limits of our identity in Purple or Blue, we can also be aware as the Red node at the same time.

Our identity (or Subjectivity) is Unconditioned Awareness (Red) of whatever arises in It.

Our identity (or Subjectivity) as Unconditioned Awareness (Red) is aware of our Energetic Presence Identity (Purple).

Our identity (or Subjectivity) as Unconditioned Awareness (Red) is aware of our Embodied Human Identity (Blue).

So whether I'm experiencing myself as a human body or as a spiritual energy, both of those experiences are aspects of my being a relative subject and both of them are experiences of myself that are happening in me as Intrinsic Awareness. Both of those are arising in "me" but by "me" I do not mean the relative subject version of "me." The relative subject is the body, the mind, and the energy, that are all arising in the "radical" or Ultimate Subject, which is Intrinsic Awareness (i.e. the Red node). Because of that, there's a kind of safety that is deeper than any threat.

This same situation applies to the Green node, too—that is, it's essential for the Ultimate spiritual dimension to be the Foundation or common ground between two or more relative subjects, so that the context of the relationship is the Ground of Being, itself. That makes a big difference in the nature of any human relationship. The reality of really meeting another human being is a frightening prospect to the relative self. It actually feels quite risky to the relative sense of self to open up to another person who appears to be objectively separate.

It's much easier to be deeply authentic with another human being if there's a sense that both of these relative subjects are arising within a larger Subjectivity that is beyond the individual relative subjects and yet is manifesting as both of them as well. Then a subtle, strange thing starts to happen, which is that the more clear I am about reality at each level, the more I can allow each level to be just what it is without needing to manipulate anything.

At first, when I became awake to the way in which we are all one as Consciousness and that there is no "other," I assumed that I didn't have to make any effort to know anyone else personally because I believed that "they are all really me, anyway." However, that assumption was based on an incomplete form of non-embodied Transcendental Divine Identity, so it didn't work very well.

Later on, it became apparent to me that—precisely because ultimately there is no "other"—I can allow you to be whatever you are. You can be different from me as a person, and I can acknowledge that I don't and really can't know who you are from your own side. I'm safe enough to allow you to be what you are because I (and you) are ultimately beyond what we appear to be but you still also exist in a relative way that I can never know. As a relative person or being, whatever you are is a mystery to me, and I don't know who you are. But whoever you may be at the relative level, there is no difference between us at the level of the Ultimate Subject of Consciousness. That's a very different understanding of Reality than pretending that variety and difference aren't real at all or that they should not be there, and saying, "we're all just one, right? We're all the same."

The relative "me" and the relative "you" are both arising in a larger Subject, and it's that Source and Context that I trust. It is confidence in "That" Ultimate Subject which grows more and more. It's not that I'm overriding my fear of "the other" as someone who may show up in some way that might be a threat to the relative "me."

Trust in the Ultimate Subject makes it possible to respect, honor and even love the relative subjects that we are, even as they are very different from each other. Then it becomes possible to actually listen to others as they are. The way in which they are one with you has nothing to do with whether they like you or even whether they agree with you; they have their own experience of reality that may be altogether different from yours. In other words, you can hear them for who they are and allow them into your world. This also applies to those in the non-human or spiritual dimensions—you can begin to let them in as well.

The thing to remember about non-embodied spiritual beings is that they are just like anybody else. I've heard it said, "Just because someone doesn't have a body doesn't mean they know more than you." Remembering this observation can be very useful.

Whatever presence I feel, I allow myself to relate to it as other and then it starts to behave as other—because I treat it as a relationship. There was a tendency at first for me to treat it all as if it were the Purple node of identity. In other words, when I felt a spiritual presence, there was energy, and so there was the sense that "it's me and my energy," even if I felt it outside my body in front of me. Well, of course, there's some truth to that, just like when I'm sitting in a circle with friends, and we're all sharing and listening to each other. When somebody speaks, I can feel the way that person is an aspect of me, too. But in the case of my friends, I also know the way that they are not me in the relative sense. There's a way in which they are me, and there's also a way in which they're not. (And there's great value in also exploring the way in which they're not me). In the way in which I'm relative, I'm relatively this, and they're relatively that and the meeting of these two "others" can be very enriching for both of us.

The same kind of relationship situation also applies to these energies: there's a way in which they're all part of my energy field and are arising in Consciousness, and there's also a way in which I can feel that presence as other than myself in the relative sense and I can allow that as a relationship.

In the shared heritage of humanity, various sacred arts and sciences have been developed for the purpose of directly working in this realm. Applying its simplest form, you can start by creating a picture in your mind to gaze at. After a while, you are able to develop an energetic communion with the internal image to such a degree that you can use it as a means for that being to contact you directly. The imaginal mind, when it's functioning consciously, has the potential to operate in both directions. That is, we can contact energetic presences (through visualization, among other ways) and they can also contact us and give us guidance through various means, such as dreams and visions, and through the feelings in our own body.

Changing Perception

The Yellow node does not look any particular way, exclusively—for some of us, it's about animal spirits, while for others, it's earth or nature spirits. Native American traditions, Japanese Shinto, and many indigenous peoples have been deeply in touch with Nature as being a community of conscious spirits. However, for the most part, these ancient understandings and capacities have been trained out of most of us.

For example, we may discount the capacity to feel the attention of other beings that are aware of us, even when we genuinely feel it.

During the middle ages, some people in Europe believed that there was something called the "light of the eyes." People took this phrase quite literally and thought that people saw things through this light, a light of visual consciousness coming out of the eyes to light up objects. They thought that was how people saw things. Of course, through science, we've learned that it doesn't work that way. There's no objectively verifiable light in the eyes that goes out and touches things.

And yet, many of us have had the experience of being "touched" by someone's attention, even before we knew they were present. It's easy to see how people would think there was a light of the eyes. When looking at things, it seems as if the substance of my attention can project from me to touch or rest on someone outside of me. In the ancient world, many people could feel the world aware of them, whether it was understood as spirits, gods, saints, or angels; they lived in a living world, and it was aware of them.

Throughout history, science has changed how people have understood reality in many ways. We've mostly forgotten how former common sense assumptions shaped people's experience and how changes in their thinking altered the very sense of reality that people had of the world around them. Today, if we include the subjective feeling of experience as a parallel reality distinct from objective reality, we can experience both. One example of this is the experience we've just described of being aware of the world being aware of you.

Later on in this chapter, we will look at reversing the flow of attention; it is a fascinating experiment that you can always do wherever you are. But first, let's examine the use of imagination and the imaginal mind and the effect it has in amplifying energy.

There's a way in which we can feel energetic presence coming towards us, and we are merely receptive. For example, we might meet a teacher, and feel a spiritual presence or energy. When you're in their presence, you contact their transmission. Also, it can sometimes happen with a loved one or an influential person in your life, that you feel their power or presence.

When you feel someone's transmission, there's a kind of registration and remembrance of that feeling. Then later, when you are no longer in their physical presence, you can use your imaginal mind to draw that transmission forward, just by thinking about the person. You can visualize them, and sometimes if you have a deep connection, you can seem to feel them being there with you. Some people experience something of this when a loved one passes. They will seem to contact the person, and if they are willing to allow the imaginal mind to function both ways, something more can happen, the experience can move from feeling communion to a communication of information.

In either case, whether sitting in silent communion or receiving communication, you can use your imaginal mind. And you can use external means to assist with this process— this is the way that some people use pictures in their spiritual practice, such as icons, or the photograph of a spiritual teacher on a shrine or in a meditation room. A picture is just a piece of paper, yet if you place a paper photo in your room and you begin to gaze at it, often the room will become filled with a transmission or presence. If you do this long enough over time, you won't even have to gaze using the picture. You'll be able to walk into the room and feel transmission. What a strange thing!

A piece of metal or ceramic shaped to represent a Buddha or a Saint will also work that way. You can sit in front of it, gazing at it, and after a while, it will act as a means of contacting presence.

Daring to Go beyond Mere Contact

We can go much further than just contacting this presence. Using ritual, prayer and visualization—all with intention to increase the feeling of the energetic presence relationship— we can pay attention to what works for us. Like building a short-wave radio or a telephone, you add the elements that create a deeper connection. It's like an internal phone—you visualize them and you can feel their presence, and you can also get the sense that they are aware of you.

In certain traditions of Hinduism, there are detailed instructions in which Temple Priests will build a statue and then empower that statue by praying for the deity that the figure represents to come into and inhabit the statue. In Tibetan Buddhism, there's a practice where you visualize in your mind a very detailed image of the deity, you imagine a very colorful living version of the divinity. Traditionally, a wall hanging, called a "thangka," of a deity like Tara or Avalokiteshvara is used as a model. These thangkas are representations of beings as experienced by people in a vision in times past. These people described them to an artist or painted the images themselves. The tradition keeps and preserves the exact details of the representation of the visionary deity and then practitioners use that vision when they visualize the deity. They also do a kind of a prayer or ritual inviting the divinity to inhabit the visualization. Not only do you—the practitioner—visualize the image in order to contact the deity that it represents, but the visualized image is also the means through which the deity represented can begin to communicate in response to you.

When the image begins to function at this other level, this is where the practice can move into devotion, and the Yellow node starts to move into Orange. When you have the sense that you could be engaging in ongoing communication through this inner "telephone," you have the feeling that "I'm contacting someone else." But it has to be understood that the context is different from the usual, everyday dualistic context. There is a sense throughout all of this, in which these deities, and Being itself, are not separate from you, they are a part of you. It's as though you are in a dream and in the dream you ask other people questions and they answer you. The other person in a dream is, of course, an aspect of your mind that is speaking to you but when you ask someone a question in a dream, and you hear the answer, you ask and listen as if they are other than you. And, the "you" in a dream is also an aspect of your mind as well.

Being conscious of this entire circumstance means having the capacity to hold the paradox of simultaneous perspectives without having one perspective invalidate the other. The beings that you contact do exist, and yet they are not ever separable from your mind.

You can see this paradox in the writings of the Tibetan practitioners. For example, many famous masters of the past directly received teachings from their chosen deities through visionary experiences, where the divinity gave the teaching.

In those traditions, it states that the source of the teachings is the Buddha or Bodhisattva who gave the instruction to the human master. At the same time, Tibetan teachers never tire of saying that it is crucial for practitioners to know that chosen deities are not external to us, but rather are intrinsically inseparable from awareness.

Outside of the Abrahamic religions of Judaism, Christianity, and Islam, there were traditions that cultivated personal revelation among those willing to do the practices. Those practitioners received teachings from these other beings directly.

Modern Western mainstream culture has very mixed feelings about the Yellow node, so it's been an uneasy dimension for most people in the West. It's a realm where anyone can claim whatever he or she pleases, so fraud abounds. As we mentioned before, it has a history of being forbidden with stories of demon possession and pacts with the devil. Worship of "other gods" is still considered evil by some and used to be a capital offense. On the other extreme, one may face ridicule for believing this is anything but deluded superstition. Finally, there is the often unspoken suspicion of madness in anyone who voices even the possibility that this realm is worth exploring. So, it takes a kind of bravery to consider this area seriously or to go into it deeply. To first be willing to contact spiritual presence is one thing, to then allow the sense that it is aware of you is deeper still, and finally to be open to personal conversation and revelation requires even more soberness and daring.

Many Westerners tend to emphasize that this kind of visionary experience is "just" your mind, maybe because it doesn't sound as superstitious, but the truth is that we are in a both/and situation here. In that sense, gods, Buddhas, bodhisattvas, saints, and angels actually do exist and can be contacted by us. The way in which they exist is accessible from a radically subjective point of view. This is a particular way of approach to this dimension. It sees that these beings are part of us, but they are functioning at a level that is beyond our relative sense of ourselves, or our identity merely as an ego.

It is also important to take note here that in addition to the way in which everyone and everything is a part of us, there is a particular way that this is true with a chosen deity. It is a step beyond contacting the many discarnate beings that can help us. A chosen deity is a representative of the One Being of which all other beings are aspects. It is the image to unify all the various aspects, and in that way it is also an image of our own Unified Self. We will look into this further in the next chapter.

The Imaginal Mind

In my view, we have severely handicapped the meaningful richness of human experience by not cultivating relationships with Presence. Everyone uses the imaginal mind, but most people do so very unconsciously. For example, when I think of my wife, I have many ideas about who she is, and there's imagery that I mentally reflect upon that affects the way that I am with her. But most of this mental activity takes place below conscious awareness. I spend lots of time with the internal image of her when I think about her, without realizing that I'm doing so.

The ability to manipulate internal imagery is an untapped capacity, an organ or "muscle" of the subtle mind that is usually quite flabby. It's an underdeveloped muscle and it's "on automatic"; we're not usually doing anything consciously to exercise it. However, the more you do use it consciously, the more it shows its potential to be a gift to us. We need to intentionally exercise our capacity to feel the livingness of the spiritual reality. We've prepared our imaginal mind to assume that everything around us is dead or nonliving. That's the underlying assumption or belief that's been conveyed to us by the secular, scientific materialist world today. The objective view of the world is valid in itself, but it isn't the whole picture. Combine this bias with the previous Christian message; "Don't be aware of the numinous presence or a universe that talks back or you may be in trouble," and you see how easy it is not to feel anything like spirit. We have blocked the flow of information and presence coming in our direction.

Because for so long we have been unconsciously and habitually using our imagination to see everything as merely non-living, dead stuff, it can now be helpful to begin to use the imagination, or the imaginal mind, in the opposite direction, with the intention to create the opposite flow. In other words, as an experiment, try using imagination in a way that's opposite to the way we've been trained.

Using the imagination to visualize is a way to start getting the energy flowing. Then, after a while, with awareness, the visualization, itself, won't be required and the energetic flow will simply be there.

EXERCISE 1: REVERSE THE FLOW OF ATTENTION

Sit down and just relax for a moment. With your eyes open in a relaxed way, see if you can become aware of the room and all the things in the room. Become aware of the presence of the room—not so much as a collection of discreet objects but the presence of the room, itself.

Now, allow yourself to experience the room as if it is being aware of you.

360 degrees, all the way around you, let it be as if the room were looking at you.

Bask in the experience of being seen.

Allowing the Experience in Different Settings

That is something to practice every once in a while, whenever you feel like it. For some people, this exercise is instantly compelling, while for others, it takes some time. Just allow yourself to use your imagination; what if the room were actually aware of me? How would that feel? Allow yourself to feel it, and pretty soon you'll experience the room being aware of you in a way that is palpable.

People feel a sense of awe when they are looking at a sunset and find themselves in communion with that spiritual energy. If you are out in nature, try allowing the trees to be aware of you, just try it out. Ancient people everywhere lived in a world that was aware of them, filled with spirits. Ultimately it was filled with One All-pervasive Spirit, and this is where the Yellow node begins to move into Orange.

You can put your attention on energetic presence at any time but certain situations—such as being at sacred places or around sacred objects—may generate the feeling more easily for you. Or a piece of art may radiate a presence. And of course, there is also the spiritual communion or energetic presence relationships with teachers or gurus, whether they are living or no longer living as their physical bodies.

When we are in communion with spiritual archetypes, such as visionary God-forms like gods and goddesses, we are moving toward pure devotion to the Supreme Presence. There, we are on the edge of Orange. Where Yellow blends into Orange, devotion is spiritual communion with the energetic presence of the Unique Divine that is all-pervading.

The mind would like to reach for dogmatic certainty about the ultimate nature of the cosmos, as a form of support. To have these images for support is fine, but they must be left behind the closer we move towards Orange, or we will simply stay with the form of support, itself. Being without a dogmatic certainty is sometimes felt as a lack, but this sort of uncertainty is a healthy thing. It's what keeps an icon from becoming an idol.

By contacting spiritual presence and feeling into it to the point that one rarely has the sense of being alone, there can be warmth, relaxation, and nurturance within presence itself, which is all surrounding and penetrating.

Three Parts of the Yellow Node

The first part of this node is Green-Yellow, where an energetic presence relationship exists in the context of a physical person, place or thing that is filled with that presence. In that situation, you come into contact with someone or something that has an active presence, vibration or transmission. Being around them, your energetic presence is stimulated by the presence or shakti of that particular physical other. Meditatively sitting with or gazing with another person, particularly a spiritual teacher, is a typical example of that.

The second part is where there is energetic presence relationship in the context of being directly in communion with a presence, itself. There may still be a person or picture associated with the transmission, but you are in communion with the energy, itself, more than with the physical person or thing associated with it. The physical aspect is just a means to connect with the energy or presence, itself.

And then there's the third part, which is Yellow-Orange. Here, the energetic presence relationship exists in the context of recognizing every instance of energetic presence as being a different aspect of the One Divine Energetic Presence. From this recognition, there is another recognition that follows having to do with the nature of your internal guidance and your own identity, which we will look at when we come to the Orange node.

Just as Red and Purple rely on each other, and Blue and Green rely on each other, Yellow and Orange also rely on each other. The nature of Yellow-Orange will be examined in the next chapter as a continuation of the thread we started here.

Recognition of One Strand begins to touch the Orange node

In the third part of the Yellow node, three things combine 1) our unique perspective and aloneness 2) the feeling of all-pervasive presence and 3) the recognition that you are receiving communication through various means. This experience is somewhat inexplicable.

Once this combination occurs, we are communing with presence, but are in a distinctly unique ongoing relationship with the Divine. This includes revelation, awe, and worship.

We're now touching the Orange node, and at this point, there is a direct recognition that all of the energies are various aspects of One Divine Energetic Presence.

The more we allow ourselves to be open to other beings as part of the One Presence that is living all beings, we may begin to experience that One through them all.

At times, different people and things will seem to be colluding in delivering a message to us. It is only we who can see or hear what they convey, and they may appear to have nothing to do with each other except to us. We can discover a unity in different things that are happening to us, and this can be revealed to us as a single message, though not necessarily from only one messenger or source. At other times we simply receive a clear, direct message. These messages come to us from the Supreme Being through pretty much anything and everything. Life circumstances, other people, animals, dreams, visions and discarnate beings can be messengers to us. The word "angel" literally means messenger.

This is the aim of devotion: to be in a relationship with the Divine That Is Beyond all the messengers but uses them. This is especially important to remember while working with spiritual teachers. Voltaire has written that "if God did not exist, it would be necessary to invent him." That is true even in this case. It's not that we have to know what the ultimate nature of the Divine is, or see the Divine in a particular way, but instead, it's crucial that we understand that the ultimate source of our guidance is beyond any guru, teaching, Dharma or religion that we follow. God may use any or all of these to guide us at certain times, but the source of guidance is beyond these. Otherwise, if at some point we find any of these lacking we may doubt our connection to the Divine, rather than learning from our experiences.

All of the means through which messages and Divine communication come are icons through which the Divine Light shines, as icons they are honored and loved, But the Beloved can take any form and is beyond every form.

EXERCISE 2

Think of a sacred image of someone or some being that you trust and that you feel is powerful for you.

When you're ready, close your eyes. Contemplate for a moment what you know about your sacred image, and allow yourself to see this image in front of you. Whatever visible attributes your sacred image has, see them. Whatever audible aspects your sacred image has, hear those. Allow whatever feelings these images and sounds produce in you to build, and allow their presence to affect you in whatever way feels safe for you.

Pay attention to what you're feeling and as you're imagining or visualizing this image, use the flow of feelings to see what qualities to enhance in your own feelings. Whatever feels better to amplify, turn it up, as if you're an artist. Try making the color brighter or making it softer and see what happens. You intuit what to do, perhaps bringing the image closer or further away, making it calm-faced or smiling. Just do whatever produces more feeling for you, more of an energetic presence. Even a nature scene can evoke a different feeling if the colors are sharper or more diffuse or if the sun is brighter.

While you're imagining your sacred image being present in front of you, just feel the presence of the image. If you can imagine the image clearly that's great, but if you can't, that's okay too; just feel the presence of the image. That's what's important, it's not necessary to be able to get a crystal clear picture, just that you feel it. When you're ready, open your eyes.

See Where We Are

So, when Sariputra heard the story of Amitabha's pure land, he was fascinated by that Buddha's awe-inspiring majesty, but then the thought came to him, "If a Buddha land is pure because of a pure mind, is it because the mind of this Buddha was not pure that this world is so unclean as we see it now?" In other words: "Well, what about you, Master? Why did you manifest this kind of a realm? It would be so much nicer to be in one of those amazing pure ones."

The Buddha knew of Sariputra's thought and said to him: "Are the sun and the moon unclean when a blind man does not see their cleanliness?"

Sariputra replied, "No Lord, this is the fault of the blind man, not that of the sun and the moon."

At that moment, the Buddha touched his big toe to the ground, and the world was suddenly transformed. It was adorned with hundreds and thousands of rare and precious gems of thousands of worlds, like the precious Majestic Buddha's pure land adorned with countless precious merits, which the assembly praised as never seen before. Also, each person present found himself seated on a precious lotus throne.

Then, the Buddha said, "Sariputra, do you see this splendor of the virtues of the buddha-field?"

Sariputra replied, "I see it, Lord! Here before me is a display of brilliance such as I have never before heard of or beheld!"

The Buddha said: "This Buddha land of mine is always pure, but appears impure." The Buddha then lifted his big toe from the ground, and the world returned to its previous condition. "Sariputra, this land is always pure, but you just don't see it."

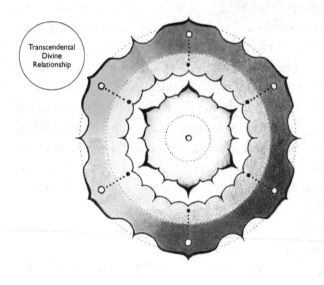

Transcendental
Divine
Relationship

Chapter 7

Devotion: Your Unique Relationship with Your Unique Deity

Orange: Transcendental Divine Relationship

In this chapter, we'll look at devotion in the context of inclusive non-duality and Radical Subjectivity. We'll return to the context of the Great Chain of Being and see how it relates to your hidden twin and devotion, altogether.

So now, let's begin where the Yellow node moves into the Orange node.

In Chapter 1 we said:

If you cultivate awareness of these diverse Energetic Presence Relationships, you may begin to recognize all energy as something you can be in relationship to as if in one single relationship.

This leads us into the realms of worship and devotional traditions. Yellow into Orange goes into Transcendental Divine Relationship, and that is relationship with the All-Pervading: The Being that is being everything. You begin to relate to the energy of the universe as a single lover or beloved.

The Orange node is about awakening to Transcendental Divine Relationship. Devotion is your unique relationship with your unique divine.

The Orange node is your experience of God (or Goddess) as

you understand and experience that One in your life. This is the realm of devotion to the Divine Person in the particular way they reveal themselves to you. Just as in an ongoing relationship with a friend or lover, you are in a special relationship where you can get to know them in a way no one else does. *All forms of prayer and acknowledgment of synchronicities become reminders that there is only one Beloved with whom you are in a private dance. Here, you open to and acknowledge the Source of Guidance in your life that is always present and personal to you.*

Like human love, the ultimate relationship is about heart and feeling communion. There are many different traditions related to the node of Transcendental Divine Relationship. Some mystical devotional paths emphasize the way in which we are embedded in and dependent upon the Divine. We are in the position of surrender. We become transformed by the reception of grace. We become holy and even divinized through participating in the energies of God.

So, while there's a way in which the Divine is never separate from us, there's also a way in which the Divine is simultaneously distinct from us. Devotion needs "two" in order for there to be the current of love, yet for non-dual devotion this is a paradox.

In India, there are both approaches: Identifying with God and worshipping God. There are those who say that we are God, there are those who worship God, and there are those who do both. One of the phrases that's well known among Indian devotees is; "I don't want to be chocolate. I want to taste chocolate." In other words, you need to be separate from the Divine in order to love the Divine.

And yet, the more you love All-pervading Presence, the more you find yourself in communion with it, and the more the sense of separation disappears. It's an ecstatic merging with the Supreme Power. Devotional mystics often use a sexual metaphor when speaking of this merging where Orange turns into Red. Relationship with Divine Radiant Presence outshines and absorbs everything else: As we move beyond words, there is non-dual dissolution. At this point, it is the coral zone, approaching the Red node of Transcendental Divine Identity.

It's Okay to Be Shy

When I've taught about devotion, I've often found myself moving in a territory beyond the mind, and beyond my capacities no matter how well I've prepared. The subject is so non-linear; it's just not the kind of subject that you can easily explain. So, I'm going to approach it here primarily from my heart.

I'll begin by saying that, for many of us, devotion may be something we're shy about. In our 21st-century modern culture, devotion can be considered either naïve or lowbrow. So, for many people, there can be a sense of embarrassment around any Energetic Presence Relationship (Yellow node) or Transcendental Divine Relationship (Orange node) experiences.

Even among folks who are "spiritual but not religious," devotion is often the poor cousin. Hatha yoga, meditation, and mindfulness are more respectable and non-threatening to modern sensibilities. The more transcendent non-dual practices like Self-inquiry are understood as being higher and more sophisticated—not for simpletons, as devotion is. So, devotion is often something that we're hesitant and embarrassed to admit that we feel an attraction to, because to many people, it seems like fantasy.

Wounds and Numbness

In the last chapter we explored the taboo about directly receiving any communication, information or hearing the voice of a deity. For some of us, even if we mechanically repeat the name of deity as a form of meditation it may be considered pretty strange, but if we do it with devotion and feeling, it can seem even weirder. And receiving an answer back would be worse still.

There can be much wounding and fear around devotional spirituality, so we need to acknowledge that and address it at the start. Many people have abused us in the name of God. Many of us were repressed in the name of what it says in the book, or what it says according to this or that church—and that can leave scars.

In the Christian world from at least 415 AD (Hypatia of Alexandria) to 1782 (Anna Goeldi) you could be burned as a witch if you were accused of heresy or demon possession. Also, there was the possibility of being accused of madness that got you locked away into a miserable existence until you stopped experiencing such things (or at least, stopped talking about them).

Over a thousand years of this has had psychological repercussions. Even if we don't consciously realize it, deep down—down to our bones—we can feel there is a safety issue.

So, for centuries it was required that we go through the motions of calling on God or praying to a saint or angel but we must go through those motions in such a way that even when we give our all, we are to expect no direct answer unless it fully accords with the way the authorities thought we should receive an answer. Anything else was dangerous. Therefore, the sane thing to do was to never open oneself to anything like personal guidance. Eventually, of course, we lost our ability to be in touch with personal contact or guidance. In our contemporary time, the idea that you would ever get a personal clear answer may be considered delusion, fantasy, or madness, and we may think that to believe otherwise is ridiculous.

We've been conditioned to numb our capacities, to not find our guide, our inner guru, our spiritual guidance. Even within ourselves—at the level of our own Energetic Presence Identity (Purple node), where we're in touch with our own sense of presence or shakti—it was risky.

But it was far more dangerous to go into Yellow and Orange territories where you have the experience of receiving messages that appear to originate from some "Other." So, very unconsciously, to a large degree, we've shut down our bodies and our energy systems without realizing it, in order to protect ourselves, to stay safe. That's one thing. Also, the idea that you actually can receive messages is greatly in doubt. There is a conspiracy of doubt, which—in this context—is another way to keep ourselves safe. So, understandably, there may be some embarrassment to suggest or believe such a thing.

Religious Narrowness

Yet, there are also people who are living another way, who are doing all that they've been conditioned to do as religious people, which is to put your whole heart into being devotional to a God Who answers you—but only in the approved fashion. If you want to know what He says, you have nothing but the revealed scriptures of your tradition.

There may be words from authorities to the effect that you have a personal relationship with God, but it's understood that this personal relationship must be in alignment with what they say the book teaches. So, the dead letter rather than the living spirit is your only approved source of revelation.

It is considered a good thing to be devoted as described in those scriptures, but the idea that spirit would speak to you and say something unique to you is not okay. Traditionally, you are encouraged to speak to God, but it may not be acceptable to receive a unique or different answer, or to see God differently than from the approved theology.

So, it's understandable if you might feel that being devoted amounts to being enslaved. The idea that you're giving yourself up, giving your autonomy away, is the other thing that people fear, and rightfully so.

A Different Approach to Devotion

In my own awakened life, I found myself reclaiming devotion differently. Perhaps ironically, the way that I hold and experience devotional spirituality now makes it the single most individuating factor in my life. So, the dimension that gives me the most autonomy as a person is the dimension that had the opposite effect when I was younger. Devotion can be the ultimate in individuation because devotion involves listening to the guidance that is the deepest "you." It's beyond your thinking mind and is experienced by you as coming from other than what you ordinarily think of as "me."

The non-dual devotion that I teach honors the way that you are contacted by a unique version of the Divine in a universe that only you, personally, experience. Having the courage to see that unique version of the Divine and having the skill to truly honor it while paradoxically maintaining appropriate relationships with other human beings is what is needed in order to successfully navigate this terrain. Staying related to other human beings in such a way that you don't negate or overrule their perspective or experience with your own experience or perspective is an appropriate conduct and bearing for devotees. Respect for others is of the utmost importance.

The Orange node needs to have room for the meeting of the conceptual and the non-conceptual. It can be amazingly fulfilling and enriching, and I want to encourage anyone who may be hesitant about publicly acknowledging their version of devotion to share it with open, sympathetic friends.

I realize that I may be using words and notions that can automatically turn certain people off. For some, the very words "God" or "Goddess" are enough to do that.

This node needs room. There are many ways that words and imagery point to things beyond themselves, and so these need not be viewed as false or merely fantasy. This territory is not literal or linear, so we use the words that we have— inadequate as they may be—even as they reveal our limitations regarding our ability to express things. In this picture, I want to embrace the many ways that the Transcendent has made itself known through archetypical and symbolic forms and to validate them as expressions of individuals and cultures throughout time. At the same time, I also have my own distinct but open underlying framework, worldview, and metaphysics, which I'll do my best to convey here.

So, of course, questions arise in this realm. For example, what is God? What, exactly, are these different spiritual beings? What are angels? What are Buddhas and Bodhisattvas? How can the images of different cultures—or of different religious "brands"—fit together? Can they even fit together at all? I'm not giving a definitive answer to these questions, and yet I do want to convey my own sense of understanding of this. The Tapestry is a schema, framework, template, or a way

of orienting to all this experience such that you have an interface with it all without your life looking like anyone else's.
What you're relating to, ultimately, is the Mystery, and the
form that it takes in your life will be yours.

Baby and Bathwater

I've gone to places in the United States where people are singing Indian spiritual songs like Kirtans or Bhajans. So many
fellow Westerners are singing to Krishna, Ram, Hanuman,
Siva, and Ganesh. I've checked with many of these folks and
they don't necessarily literally believe the details of stories
of these divinities, nor do they follow the rules of traditional
Hinduism. But they happily sing songs that open their hearts
and touch their own inner divinity.

I often wondered, "What would happen if we all started
singing to Jesus?" I have a feeling that those people might re-
act very negatively and perhaps even with hostility. When it
comes to something so close to home, with so many uncomfortable associations, the response may be, "Can't do that.
Not that one."

This is understandable because of the past. But I'd like to
reclaim what I can of that. In some ways, we are "throwing out
the baby with the bath water." For me, being able to salvage
our traditions can be deeply enriching.

Many spiritual relationships that are precious to us may
not fit into a framework of spirituality that is consistent with
common understanding—but the Tapestry doesn't have to
fit logically and linearly. There may be whole pieces of orthodox Christianity that we don't agree with and because of that
we reject devotion to Jesus, Mary or Saint Francis, thinking,
"Well, these saints are associated with all of that." And yet,

that situation can also be true of Hinduism if you approach it as a monolithic creedal religion. Very few individuals in the West would agree with the caste system, but they still may honor gods that, in India, have been associated with the caste system and with other traditions that they feel are not valid. There are all kinds of objectionable things in traditions all over the planet.

However, having relationships with these beings doesn't necessarily mean that we have to take on every aspect of a culture that, traditionally, has been associated with them. Instead, we should claim the freedom to deepen and nourish and allow ourselves to get the blessing power and help that comes through devotion to that deity or saint. That is part of our heritage as human beings. It's part of our lineage as humanity. It is important to claim the heritage of humanity as a whole as we feel moved.

We can all reclaim precious pieces of ancient ruined buildings that are thousands of years old that may have been associated with tremendous achievements, things of beauty—but also with horrific things. And we can still be happy to be part of a history that belongs to us all, preserving what is valuable in it.

Archetypical Images

There are many ways to think about the use of spiritual imagery. In one sense, using spiritual imagery is a way of drawing down, communing with and embodying energies. For example, Jung teaches about archetypical forces (or patterns) in all human beings that he says are in the "collective unconscious." These patterns make themselves known to our conscious minds through archetypical images. The work of integration is the recognition of these archetypical forces as parts of us that we can consciously actualize. From this perspective, these forces seek to be expressed in our lives as we are individualized through their embodiment, becoming a more authentic, self-determined person by their integration. Archetypical images here act as a means to access the impulses of our being.

Jung was known for living on the interface between ancient mystical teachings and modern psychological understanding. By describing the collective unconscious as structures of the unconscious mind shared by the entire human species, he leaves room for a biological view where the archetypical patterns can be seen as mental instincts. So that's one way of holding all this.

Chosen Deities

A similar but more explicitly spiritual approach is expressed in teachings of the East. In Advaita Vedanta, there is the practice of having an "Ishta Devata" which is your personal chosen deity. From this perspective, the formless Brahman (Ultimate Reality) can be approached by the human mind using a particular form of God, which is a version of God with whom you can have a personal relationship to purify your heart and concentration. In Tibetan Buddhism, a Yidam (pledge being) is a deity with whom you form a bond such that you receive their blessings and eventually identify with them to the point of merging with and even becoming that being.

The understanding here is that many different forms can be used to approach what is essentially one truth beyond all the forms. Depending on the person, a specific form may be appropriate, but any image of a deity or teacher that you consider Divine—even an emblem or symbol of the Divine, could be a means for you in this way.

The Yellow node includes the use of deities or archetypical images—whether you think of them as God Almighty or messengers of God or angels or Buddhas or Bodhisattvas—because those are all examples of Energetic Presence Relationship. The designation "chosen deity" can be a bit misleading because the experience can often be that the divinity chooses you rather than the other way around. In some cases the image or being may even make itself known in dreams or visions.

Usually, we are familiar with these images from religious traditions or the art and literature of ancient mythologies. Seeing them may call forth something in us, or produce a sense of recognition of a quality or attribute that we're attracted to, or want to develop. The way to work with this imagery is to follow your heart and pay attention to what you feel. If you feel attracted to the image, if you find yourself feeling a presence of love while seeing the image, these are indicators of a good fit for you.

The Attributes of Distinct Deities

There is a magnetic quality to the deity itself, and the relationship is alchemical, it changes you. It catalyzes and stimulates the qualities in you that the divinity represents and in some sense IS. Being attached to that particular beloved, in devotion to its essence, the very feeling of attraction is drawing out from yourself your own hidden attributes. It awakens and pulls forth something from within us. There is a harmonic resonance between something we're attracted to and ourselves. It's a bond created that eventually becomes a kind of resonant feeling of expansion, a sense of authentic self. Through this, we feel the sense of an individuated, divine person-ness, a nectarous quality of our particular soul.

From my perspective, that is the same thing as incarnating those attributes that are the deity. The qualities that are in the deity when you're in harmonic resonance, and when you're feeling it, eventually become incarnated in and as you, as your sense of yourself. You begin to embody those very attributes. So, for example, if you are moved by Quan Yin—the female form of the Bodhisattva of compassion—then in some sense you are recognizing Quan Yin, and honoring her in that recognition. If you sit with her and develop a relationship with that archetypical image and spend time and honor that resonance you feel, then you receive something from Quan Yin that transforms you.

There is a paradoxical relationship where you see the beloved as your own deeper, more authentic self that you are now incarnating. That is one way of understanding the claims of the disciples of certain past spiritual teachers that they were incarnations or emanations of traditional deities. For example, the Dalai Lama is said to be an incarnation of the male form of the Bodhisattva of Compassion.

From Yellow to Orange: From Many to the One

For those of us in the Western world, the idea of having multiple deities while still recognizing a fundamental unity of being can seem strange. Being raised in a monotheistic culture, the notion of "many deities" and "One Being" can seem an unsolvable contradiction.

In the Yellow node, deities are seen as various beings with whom you are in relationship. In the Orange node, we move into a place where we begin to see these beings as different messengers, aspects, types, examples or faces of One Being or of Being, Itself. You can treat them as separate beings, or you can see them as different aspects of One Radiant Being, depending on which node you are looking from. In different contexts, an image or deity can represent a particular quality or type or energy, but can also represent all the qualities or energies combined, or the Source of all the qualities or energies.

We always deeply honor and thank those from whom we receive transmission, and yet the divine figures or teachers in themselves are not as significant as the energies or transmissions that they represent and radiate. It is your relationship with those powers, energies or Shaktis that transforms your sense of self and this is true in both the Yellow and Orange nodes. The images, beings or teachers are the sacred means, but not the ends. We respectfully use them to contact the spiritual energies or (finally) the One Energy with which we commune and in which we become transformed.

When we recognize that the image stands for all Divinity we are clearly in Orange or Transcendental Divine Relationship. And though we may occasionally use the image, we know that it represents That which is beyond any representation. At that point—if you are working with more than one image—they are all different faces or aspects of the One. Like many rivers flowing into one ocean, all the images—and indeed all the energies behind the images—are blended into one all-pervasive Energy or Power. That blending is not motivated by any theological map, but is an experience of letting go of concepts.

In the Orange node, this direction of inclusion can continue to the point where the practitioner, the world and everything else is seen to be that One. Ultimately, we are in a relationship with the Supreme Power that is both living and being everything (including ourselves), and in that relationship, we lose our separate sense of self. At that point, communion gives way to identity, and we are bordering on the Red node, completing the Mandala.

Worship for Individuals

A crucial thing to understand is that what is revealed to you is not for everyone else. If the Divine guides you or communicates with you, this doesn't mean that anyone else needs to do what you say. In other words, you're not a prophet, and the communication you received is not necessarily given for anyone other than yourself. It's not the complete truth—we are given information on a "need to know" basis. That doesn't mean you can't share it, but whatever is shared is not binding on other people.

This understanding clears up many things so well that the questions about which picture of the cosmos is "the correct one" tend to fall away. Every kind of revelation uses the particular form or messenger that is appropriate to the person who receives the message, and every message is specifically for them.

Coming to this particular understanding was a major turning point for me. While it had been percolating for years, it is only during the past ten years or so that this has really crystallized into something obvious to me. Strangely, and perhaps ironically, the clarity came while reading about Islamic mysticism—in particular, the teachings of Ibn Arabi. During that time, I came across an affirmation of experiences I had been struggling with for many years.

Ibn Arabi had his own thorough understanding and honoring of individuality, nonduality, and devotion. Arabi was a practicing Muslim who lived in 13th century Islamic Spain. He had access to near Eastern, Greek, Egyptian, Jewish and Christian mysticism. Al-Andalus or Andalusia—the Muslim Kingdom of Spain—was quite open, intellectually. It may have been the most open Muslim kingdom that ever existed regarding its relationships with Christians and Jews. Arabi seemed to consider that, in a certain sense, the Sufi teaching was the esoteric tradition of all revealed religion. When I began to get a sense of the way he approached devotion, I was astonished at how he understood the intrinsic value of the individual person.

Things that had happened to me throughout my life, starting from my youth, were being described using the language of a culture and time that was not my own, but it fit my experience precisely.

As I understand Ibn Arabi, every friend of God can continue to have the kind of direct guidance that the prophets received. Anyone who is mystically inclined can be in the same sort of relationship with God that a prophet was, but unlike the way it was with the prophets, what is revealed now to someone is not binding upon other people. This means that when you receive a revelation, it isn't for anyone else. Prophets have already come to all the peoples of the earth, and every distinct culture now has its moral codes, so there's no need for prophets in that sense. The personal relationship with God is always available to anyone who turns to God and cultivates it. So, you can indeed receive revelation from God, but it comes to you uniquely and is for no one else.

The way in which revelation is given is in the form of an epiphany or a theophany. According to Islam, Mohammad received his revelation from Gabriel. Although it was a revelation from God, it was given through the angel. Moses, according to Judaism, received his revelation through the angel in the burning bush. The revelation was given to Moses from God but it was God in the form of a burning bush. Abraham received a message from God while having a meal with some strangers who came by for a visit. The message comes to you through a messenger or vehicle of some kind. The word "angel" literally means "messenger" in Greek and Hebrew.

God comes to people in different ways, through a unique event or form. For some people, it happens in dreams or visions. For other people, it comes through teachers or situations in which they suddenly realize that God is speaking to them through someone or some situation. When you have this experience, you find that wherever you are at that moment, you are now on holy ground and something is being revealed to you, personally. It could happen that no one else is a witness. Whoever is involved is a messenger and their word—at least at that moment—is God's word (even if they, themselves, don't know it). It can also happen that God reveals something to you through a situation, so at that moment the situation, itself, is the messenger or angel. This kind of revelation always transmits the Unity or Single intelligence of all things even as it gives whatever information it does. The very means that is used is, itself, the greatest revelation. That is the way in which revelation is given in the form of an epiphany or a theophany.

For our own part, we can develop increasing sensitivity in our own energetic presence (the Purple node) to the point where we feel and contact our guidance and honor it. Then we take part in Energetic Presence Relationships (the Yellow node) of different kinds, being led where our energy is nourished. When we recognize that there is One Guide Who is using all the many forms of guidance that we receive, we see that they are all messengers from the same Source and we are then in the Orange node. From this place of recognition, you receive directly from your angel, from your unique face of God.

Revisiting the Great Chain of Being

As we mentioned earlier, The Tapestry nodes are similar to the metaphysical picture traditionally referred to in mystical traditions as a "great chain" or "ladder" of Being. Reality, as we experience it from the Radically Subjective perspective, is a kind of unpacking and unfolding of the potential within the formless Absolute through a process of emanation. This is akin to the way that a dream arises in the midst of deep sleep.

We can see this as if each level (or node) arises from within the one before it, like a telescope. The Radically Subjective basis of experience is the Red node of Transcendental Divine Identity. In it, all possible experience exists only as potential. In this content-free space—the Ground of everything—there is nothing and no separate one to experience anything. There is only the Silence of Emptiness.

And yet, this Empty silence is not dead like a vacuum. Rather, it is the Source of every appearance that arises. It is full of pure potential, and its nature is Intrinsic Awareness. It is Awareness that is full of pure potentiality.

The Purple node of Energetic Presence Identity is the coming forth of that pure potentiality as the fundamental object of Awareness, the feeling of being: The sense of "I-Am," itself.

In the language of Hindu Śaivism, the Red node is Shiva, and the Purple node is Shakti (power), but we should remember that the two are never really separated. Shiva is always aware of Shakti and Shiva cannot experience anything except through Shakti or power.

Within that infinite Red, a vast humming field of energy arises that is a sea of I-ness, The "I-Am" feeling itself. Within this vast power, there are countless qualities and attributes in latent potential, and there are infinite ways of combining these that form all possible experience: the "Dance of Shiva."

From this perspective, the Dance of Shiva (which is all experience) is the inherent freedom in the Energy (Shakti) of the universe. Through the Dance of the Universe, there is experience of which to be aware, through which God knows Itself in its infinite variety.

In the Sufi language of Ibn Arabi, the Absolute is the unknowable, unspeakable, eternal One—the Ground of Being which is beyond every concept. Within God—the Unknowable—was the unknown potential that yearned to be seen. All of the Names or attributes of God were a hidden treasure that desired to be known, so the first manifestation was to bring forth "The Cloud" of mercy in which all of the creation was to be made. Creation, itself, is an act of compassion for that potential that yearned to be seen.

Now, what is our Blue node experience in this unfolding? As Embodied Human Identity, we are in each moment a particular finite form that appears to exist entirely distinct from all other creatures. This feeling of being a body/mind, a different form cut off and separate from everything else we see so that it appears as "not me" is the further revealing of the potential that is hidden in the Energetic Presence. As a separate body/mind that is distinct from its environment, we exist with the sense of death and limits: the vulnerability at the heart of life.

Blue is an unpacking of the potential that is in the Purple

node in the same way that Purple is an unpacking of the potential that is in the Red node. Some qualities cannot come
forward unless there is the experience of duality. The experience of duality brings us the experience of limits and finiteness. For example, you can't experience the qualities of compassion and love unless there is some sense of another. Those
qualities were only in seed form in the prior nodes and needed both manifestation and the distinct felt sense of duality in
order to come into existence and be experienced.

For one who is living the Tapestry, there is the paradox of
being all three of these identities simultaneously. There is the
way in which there is no "you" or "them" at all—that is to say,
everything is just an appearance in Unconditioned Awareness (Red). And yet, at the same time, there is the awareness
both of the way in which other beings (and things) are separate and distinct from you (Blue) and also of the way in which
they are not separate from you (Purple).

Regarding experience, there are always two levels: one in
which we are one with all of our environment through the
current of non-separateness permeating everything, and the
other in which we are distinct individuals unable to truly
know anyone else or to be known by anyone else. That finiteness is precisely our uniqueness. We often think of the body/
mind as being "in" the universe that we see, but actually, it is
simply the most local aspect of that universe, it is the universe
as us.

Paradoxically, the universe as ourselves—the body/mind
itself—presents us with a version of the world that is unique
to us. We are certainly aware of other sentient beings, and
we make reference to common sight and sounds, but we are
never actually experiencing things in exactly the same way as
anyone else nor even experiencing exactly the same things.

What we see as we look into this universe, is a world that no one else sees. This recognition reveals us to be very alone. Even without this level of awareness, we feel alone, but we don't know why. Friends are wonderful, but they will never see through your eyes.

With this clarity, we can acknowledge that the way we are experiencing a "shared" universe is very different from the way we usually think about it. The two ways we see the world do not cancel each other out. There's a way in which I look at the universe and I see myself. My body is not "in" the universe but is an opening into the universe. It's as if my eyes are positioned to look "inside" and I am looking into my own larger body/mind. As in a dream, everything I see is myself. And yet, regarding the appearances that arise, I am at the same time simply one person relating to everyone and everything else, and in that way, they are not me at all. They are their own distinct persons, ultimately as unknown to me as I am to them. Embodied Human Relationship (the Green node) is an honoring of both of these dimensions and opens an intimacy founded on attentiveness and mystery.

In the Green node, we are honoring both the experience of non-separateness (Purple dimension) and the experience of separateness (Blue dimension) in the context of relationship. Even the limitations of Blue are an unfolding of potential qualities that were latent in the Purple dimension, and it is through those limitations that we contact another sort of connection, one that includes the sense of "other." What makes the veil of duality a delusion is that it seems to separate the body/mind from its environment. In the mystery of the appearance of duality arising in non-duality, the sense of separateness reveals hidden qualities while it simultaneously veils wholeness. The perspective of the Tapestry of Being is an "inclusive" non-duality, from this view, even the sense of duality is never some sort of mistake, but rather is a revealing and experiencing of the potential in the un-manifest.

Your Higher Self Is a Portion of Purple

As we move further into the relationship nodes, the question of who, exactly, it is that we are in relationship with becomes more interesting. In anticipating the Orange node, we can see the way that there is One Intelligence speaking through many messengers. And yet, that One Intelligence is, Itself in a private relationship with us.

This brings me to what may be the most challenging piece of the view to convey: The relationship between our guidance and our world, and the nature of our incarnation as an individual soul.

As I mentioned earlier, each soul is a singular or unique point of view. As a singular point of view, it sees a single world that is known by no one else. Both you and your world are a continual emanation and incarnation of Purple node energies becoming apparently separate forms. This is what our lived life is. What I'd like to add here is the notion that regardless of how long your life is, or how many lives you lived, we would never experience enough to exhaust the potential of the Purple node.

This is the juncture of Purple and Blue where the limits of form become known. Our entire lives are always only a portion of the infinite attributes, qualities and flavors that could be manifested. Although we cannot know the experience of the countless beings that have lived, they have each experienced a unique manifestation and combination of the potential that unfolded as their lives.

Both you and the world you see are an emanation of that branch or river of the energies of the Divine that contain the particular qualities or attributes that comprise you and your experienced world. That one continuous event (you and your world) has two poles: your point of view (soul) and the invisible Intelligence that is in all you experience. The all-pervasive Intelligence of your unique world is your unique guide or unique face of God. It underlies the world you experience and in the Radically Subjective sense, directs all. It is the Soul of your world and is behind the synchronicities that you are aware of, but which other people will never objectively see. You are in continual relationship with that singular face of God. You are alone with The Alone.

To recognize your life as the unfolding of the specific experiences necessary to incarnate and manifest the particular matrix of qualities that you are to embody is to incarnate the distinct face of the Divine that is your higher self.

Called to the Source through Relationship with the Unique Divine

At the level of the Red node, I am simply the Unconditioned Awareness of whatever is. And yet, in my experience as a distinct being in life, my soul's perspective is a particular manifestation of the Supreme Power that arises in Unconditioned Awareness. If as a soul, I am an emanation or manifestation of the Power of the Universe, then I am a part and parcel of that Power, as is everything I perceive.

In the Yellow node it's as though our own particular Energetic Presence Identity reaches back towards us to contact us through, and as, apparent others in relationship. When there is the sense that this is always a singular relationship despite appearances, this is the Orange node, and it can lead to a radiance that outshines the distinctions.

There are many versions of this picture throughout the ancient world. Myths try to convey it, but it escapes being pinned down by language, though poetry can come near.

The Divine that reaches out to us is a unique face of God, a distinct messenger. In essence, it is a fuller Energetic Presence version of ourselves that is the river from which we are incarnating. That current of Energetic Presence that manifests you and your world exists as "a larger You" and a "Higher" self. In Gnostic traditions, this is known as your "Twin," "Angel," and "Guide." It is also the version of yourself that you are longing to embody and manifest in your earthly life.

This inner teacher or guru is also your ideal future spiritual self. If you think about what you would ideally be—whether many lives from now or maybe even at the end of this life, with all the divine attributes that you could possibly have—that's the unique version or face of God that is your guide.

That future self is present even now, as your shepherd. It's pulling you forward into itself. It's creating all the circumstances and situations that are necessary for you to bring forth and embody those qualities. It is leading you to become itself. It is that which shows the path, it is the path itself and it is the destination. A significant part of this process is recognizing that guidance. Then there is also being in devotional communion with it, as all that is, and beyond.

The particular world that you experience is a manifestation of that portion of the Supreme Power that also manifests as you. When you go to sleep, your version of the world sleeps, and when you awaken, it also awakens. You and your world are both manifested in and by the same unique Matrix of Energy, and that is why your guide can use anyone and any situation to call attention to Itself and lead you. That Higher Self is you and all that you experience. It is not the formless silent "Self" of Unconditioned Awareness (Red node) but rather your invisible personal guide or deity, the still small voice calling you forward, your other half that has never left the Energetic Realm.

Knowing this is a different issue from knowing your nature beyond form. It is rather the capacity to be sensitive to how your body/mind is to be used by Being in your particular life. When Sri Ramana Maharshi awoke as the Self, it was a Red node event. When he later heard the call to live with his Guru—the mountain Arunachala, which he took to be Siva—it was a Yellow node event. When he then sat "at the feet" of his Mountain and wrote hymns, it was an Orange node event. All three nodes are paradoxically compatible, although they are also distinct. The Red perspective doesn't negate the Yellow or Orange. From the Red node perspective, there was no need for Ramana to go to Arunachala, because there was nothing he needed and he was beyond seeking or going anywhere. Being in the Eternal Here and Now, where could he "go"? Yet, from the Yellow node perspective, he had to honor the pull of his heart to heed Arunachala's call. And from the Orange perspective, he sat at the feet of Arunachala and never left because of his steadfast devotion to God in that particular form, even though Sri Ramana saw God in every form.

We need to pay close attention to where we are being led, individually. Our inner leadings are such an individual thread that it doesn't depend on a particular lineage. In principle, your inner guru can use any lineage, any deity, any guide, and any master if you're able to hear and willing to follow its leading.

My own guru, H.W.L. Poonja "Papaji," was known primarily as a disciple of Sri Ramana Maharshi and as a teacher of Advaita Vedanta (a Hindu Red node teaching). I was a Buddhist practitioner, not interested in any Hindu guru, when I first came into contact with Papaji's teachings and transmission. However, when I met his disciples, the strong presence that I felt with them pulled me to meet him, myself. I had been doing Buddhist devotional practice to Padmasambhava at the shrine in my home, and as I sat before the statue of Padmasambhava, its face transformed into Papaji's. When I then went to India and met Papaji himself, the recognition and attraction spoke to my heart, despite the difference in tradition and lineage.

Although Papaji was a master of the Red node, he was also a master of the Yellow and Orange nodes. When asked if he had any relationship with The Goddess Durga—the personification of the Supreme Power of Energy (Shakti)—he replied that all masters have a relationship with Durga. He then said something that struck me deeply: "If you don't know how to feed your own energy, how will you know where to go?"

This aspect of Papaji's teaching went unnoticed by some of his students, perhaps because it seemed to contradict the uncompromising Red node teachings that Papaji also taught. Those teachings were primarily about Consciousness, so when you asked most of the people around him about experiences of energy, they would often say "Well, it doesn't matter, those are just experiences, just phenomena. It's part of Maya, it doesn't mean anything." And yet, if you'd ask those same people, "Which teachers do you like to go to see?," they'd say, "Well, I like to go to this one or that one because of the energy or grace." Because they felt a resonance, that's how they knew they were in the right place. They paid attention to the vibration that they felt.

To treat that resonance as the indicator of and ongoing relationship with your guidance is a deeper devotion. This isn't just about a particular guru; different people will resonate with different teachers or deities. Another way of describing this is as the inner guru principle that is leading you. That guru will speak through various vehicles at different times and it is to that inner guru that we must remain faithful.

Many people can be in the same room and each one have an entirely different experience of a teacher or an entirely different experience of a deity. Perhaps they are not attracted— or they may even be repulsed—because their inner guide is not using that deity or teacher as a manifestation in that person's life, so he or she is not their teacher. This invisible guide that you are in relationship with is the unique form of God that is inseparable from you, and it may use a teacher or guide with whom no one else feels anything.

The inner guru is nameless, but we often use the name of the vehicle through whom our inner guru has most fully revealed itself, and it is fitting to do so. I'll sometimes say "this is all Papaji" or "it's all Padmasambhava." In other words, you can identify a particular deity or teacher with your inner guide to such an extent that you refer to the guidance, itself, by the name of that deity or teacher, whether they're physically alive or not. This Beloved One can appear to you as either male or female but is really beyond gender. Although this guide is one and singular, it can also appear as more than one form or person in your life.

In my case, my guru is both Guru Rinpoche Padmasambhava and Papaji. After his passing, Papaji continued to lead me. That is to say, the inner guru who revealed himself to me most fully as Papaji is absolutely one with my inner guru. Papaji speaks to me through other people. It's a relationship of love. It is speaking of the heart. The inner guide is invisible and is so close to me that he or she came in the form of Papaji to talk to me and she also came in the shape of Padmasambhava. She came as Jesus at a certain point in my life and she has also come in the form of many different friends and teachers.

My inner guru—my guide, my master, my teacher—is not limited by my ideas about or my experience of the physical man, Papaji, nor by my thoughts of who Guru Rinpoche is. All the qualities I have found and continue to find attractive in the man, Papaji—as well as in Guru Rinpoche and any others who are guides for me—draw me to my own invisible Beloved, Who is the One they truly are.

That inner teacher is embedded in the Self (the Red node) and leads you to that Empty Awareness, over and over again. She or He is the Energy of that Self that acts, moves and attracts (the Purple node), and in that sense, is your own self, inseparable from the world in which you live. The Inner Beloved is, in some ways, like a conjoined twin to you, always on the other side of your experience, willing to contact you through any of the apparent others you come across, through a situation or through a vision, dream, voice, or intuition that you receive.

We live in a dualistic world that includes a relative world of which I'm a relative subject living with relative objects. In that world, we know that each person has their own truth, whether we agree or disagree with them, and we hear it as the experience or perspective of another being. Simultaneously, alongside that relative world, there is a realm of the Radical Subjective in which the whole world is an icon, where all those different voices are the means through which the Radically Subjective Guide speaks to you. This is the realm of synchronicity, the realm where everybody and everything— including beings that are in bodies and beings that are out of bodies—can all be a way in which you are contacted. In the Radically Subjective sense, the world is a way for you to be in a relationship with The Presence of the Divine Beloved, the purpose of which is to incarnate that Beloved, more and more.

Your unique version of God is inseparable from you such that it is perfectly natural for you to embody all of its qualities—but this happens only if you respond to the call of devotion. Like a lock and key, the version of the Divine that calls to you, personally, is a perfect fit for your heart. From this perspective, devotion individuates you into a uniquely integrated, authentic being who manifests the divine qualities of your higher self to the point of total identification.

Divine Heart, Fierce and Gentle

Where has it led in my case?

Years after that initiatory awakening into the Conscious nature and deep energetic embracing embodiment, what does life look like as I unravel into the feeling of authenticity?

For me, it leads to Devotion to the One who is living and being all of Life, who is mysteriously She, He, me.

It leads to the revelation of the Divine Being, in and as myself, in and as others, and in and as life itself. I'm not speaking here of any particular idea of the Divine other than the Conscious Radiant Heart of Life itself.

Trusting ourselves to Divine Being is knowing that our lives, no matter who we are, are always sustained and lived by a Power beyond the mind's ability to comprehend. We are always lived by that One, we are always living in that One and when we die, we will certainly die in that One.

The heart of devotion is the recognition of all of life as the expression of the Beloved. All of life is the Radiance of Consciousness. To see Life as the unfolding drama of both your humanity yearning to go beyond its limits and the Beloved Divine yearning to experience its limits—as your life—is to see the Love affair between God and you, as You.

It is said that The Supreme Power is without need, complete in Itself. Of course, that is true. Yet, all this Universe (and more) is the Overflowing of that Fullness. The Uncontainable Desire of this Infinite Being is Its Ecstatic Freedom to pour out and become all that it is IN LOVE.

Your own Life
Is the Overflowing Divine Desire of Radiant Consciousness
to appear
as You
and through being You
to recognize Itself
everywhere.

Its Overflowing Desire to be and know you
through experiencing you
as limits
and Its desire to be you
and in relationship with you
through and as life itself
and through and as "others" in life
Is what you—your life—is
Now.

The Heart is
strong in the confidence of unknowing
free of notions of ourselves
flowing with authentic feeling
in the warm empty sphere of clarity
not interested in conceptualizing about Who is living us
there is trust without minding
and the experience of being our truest selves
moment by moment
not knowing
or
able to say
who it is
that is
simply arising as this
but is obviously
who you are.

About the Author

Krishna Gauci was brought up in the projects of the Bronx, New York. He worked as a cab driver, an auto assembly line worker, a cabinetmaker and a city bus driver. In 1993, after more than a decade of meditating and working with teachers, he went to India and met his master HWL Poonja, which became a foundation for the rest of his life. Krishna has been teaching and assisting people with their spiritual lives since 2001. He has worked with hundreds of people in both retreat settings and individual consulting sessions. His approach is down to earth and practical, even as it points to the highest transcendence.

As a result of his exposure to many different spiritual approaches, he developed the Tapestry of Being paradigm, which bridges various traditional influences to serve 21st century people in orienting to the mystery of Being. For the past seven years, he has offered the Tapestry of Being teachings with students worldwide.

He lives with his wife Vivian in Portland, Oregon.

CPSIA information can be obtained
at www.ICGtesting.com
Printed in the USA
LVHW080834020719
622924LV00004B/14/P